# ESSENTIAL SKILLS

# ALTERNATE TUNINGS

by Matt Smith

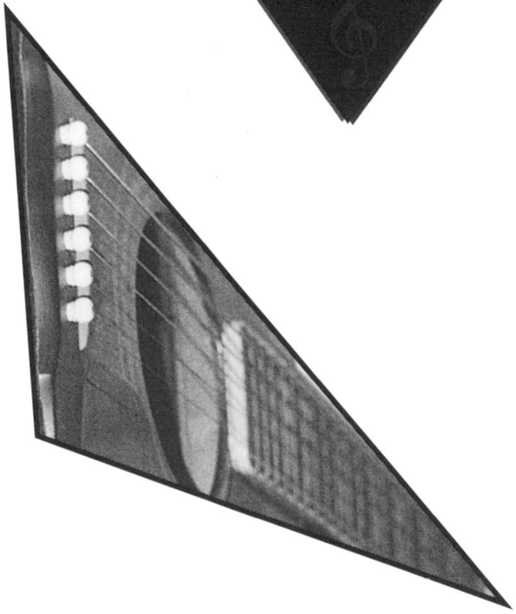

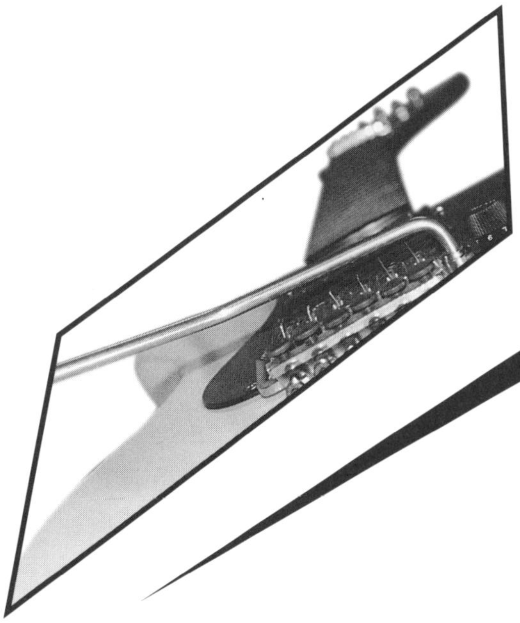

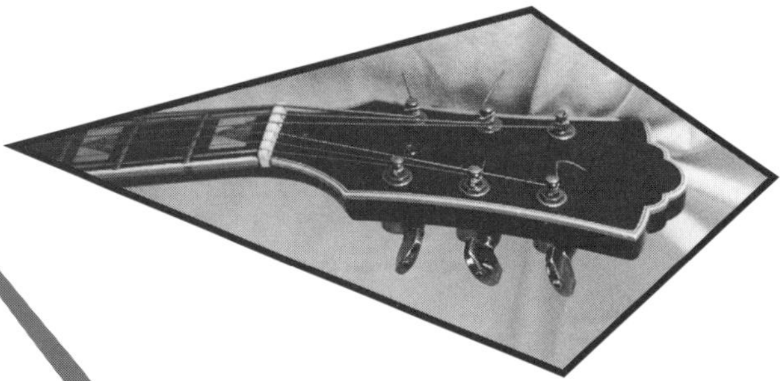

*For Rachel*

For a comprehensive listing of Cherry Lane Music's songbooks, sheet music, instructional materials, videos and more, check out our entire catalog on the Internet. Our home page address is: http://www.cherrylane.com

# Table Of Contents

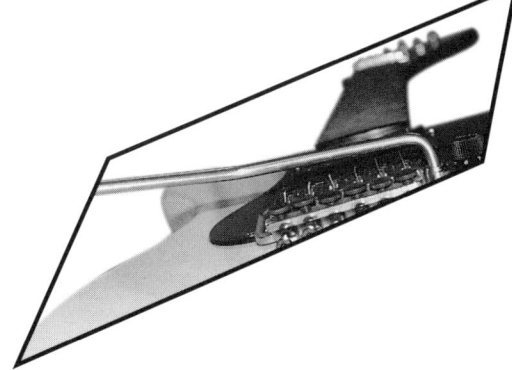

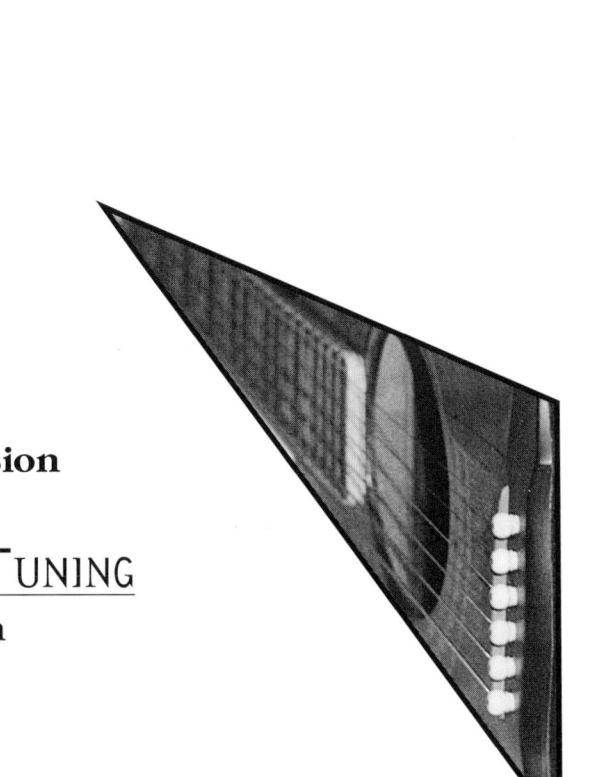

Editor's Note: All tunings are from low to high (6th to 1st string). All music is in 4/4 time unless otherwise noted.

# Introduction

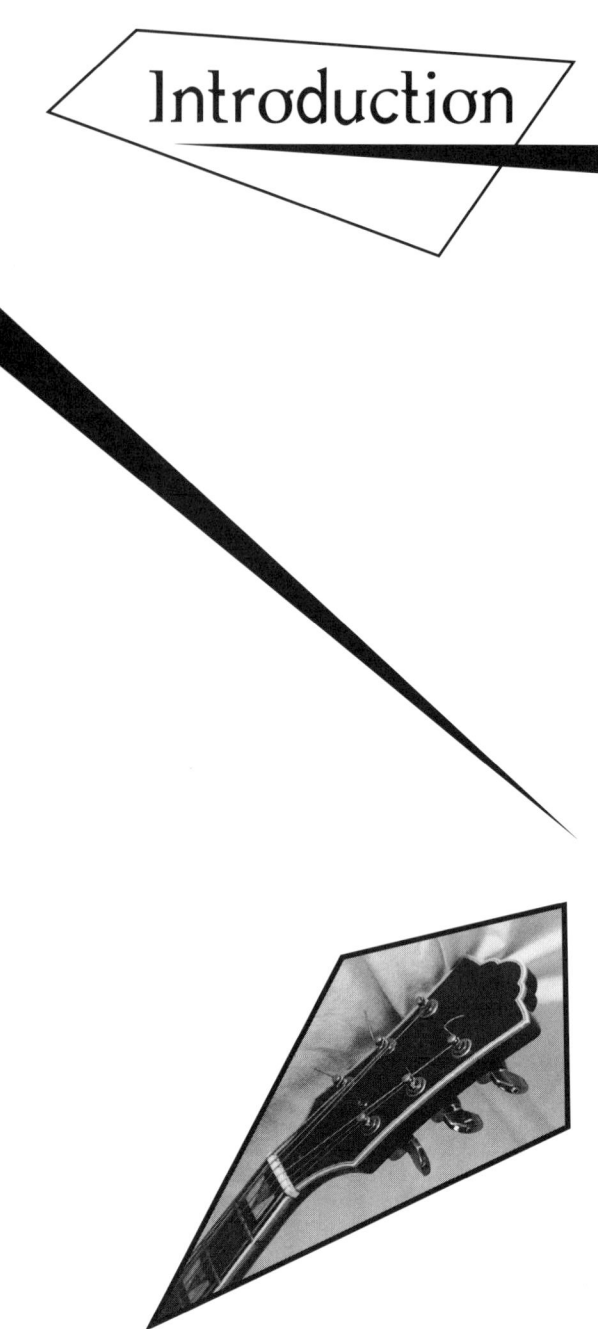

Nothing can open the floodgates of inspiration like alternate tunings. Cranking your guitar strings up to the point of breaking, or loosening them to the feel of limp fishing line, can elevate your playing to new plateaus of creativity. If you haven't used alternate tunings yet, you've been missing out on a whole world of new sounds.

This book will serve as your guide through these seemingly mysterious, uncharted waters. For the more experienced peg puller, this book will serve as a handy reference guide for exploring new tunings, and will bring a fresh perspective on some old friends.

What is now considered "standard" tuning is not by any means the original tuning for guitar. The guitar and its predecessors have undergone many different tunings, and even numbers of strings. *Scordatura*, or the retuning of a string instrument to simplify the performance of a piece of music, has been used by guitarists throughout the ages.

It is often easier to sound better in an alternate tuning than in standard tuning, particularly when tuned to a chord, such as open C, G, E or A. When you use these types of tunings (often called *open tunings*), any full-barre at any fret produces a major chord. Simple chord forms that combine fretted notes and open strings will sound uniquely ethereal.

The greatest benefit you will reap from alternate tunings is the emancipation from conventional ideas. Everything you might normally play takes on an exciting new sound when played in an alternate tuning. Don't be afraid of a little free-form exploration either; new licks, grooves and even songs will burst out from beneath your fingertips as you explore new tunings!

Keep in mind that some tunings may require different string gauges. Tuning your low-E down to B using a .42 string can leave the pitch rather dubious, and you stand little chance of tuning your high E up to an A with (what was) a .13. Try to keep various gauges of strings handy for the extremes. Also, you may have to make some minor neck adjustments if you plan to keep your guitar in a vastly altered tuning for an extended time.

This book presents dozens of useful tunings that work well for electric or acoustic guitar. The most important tunings are explored within the musical examples; in addition, we will cover the common chord and scale fingerings in these tunings, since all familiar chords and scales require new fingerings in each tuning. Song lists are provided for all tunings so that you know what tunings your favorite guitarists use. Keep an open mind, and remember that this book is a spring board for your own explorations!

# About The Author

Matt Smith is a New York City–based guitarist, singer and songwriter. An instructor at the American Institute of Guitar in Manhattan and the National Guitar Summer Workshop in Connecticut, Matt also runs guitar clinics for Ovation and Hamer guitars and Trace Elliot amplifiers. Matt and his band have performed with B.B. King, Al DiMeola, Adrian Legg, Johnny Winter, Spin Doctors and many others, and have released four albums on New Millennium Records.

**ACKNOWLEDGMENTS**

I would like to sincerely thank the following people for their invaluable assistance with this project: Rachel Cooper, Craig Geoffrey, Kevin Gray, Arthur Rotfeld, Ted Piechocinski, Jon Chappell, New Music, Sam Ash Music and Books, all at Kaman Music, and especially my parents, Alfred and Helen Smith. This book is dedicated to the memory of Jesse Dog.

# DROP D TUNING—D A D G B E

(Tune the 6th string down a whole step.)

This alternate tuning is the simplest and most common, used in virtually all styles of music. If you're in the key of D, it doesn't make much sense to leave that all-important 6th string tuned to E—crank it down to D!

## D MAJOR SCALE DIAGRAM

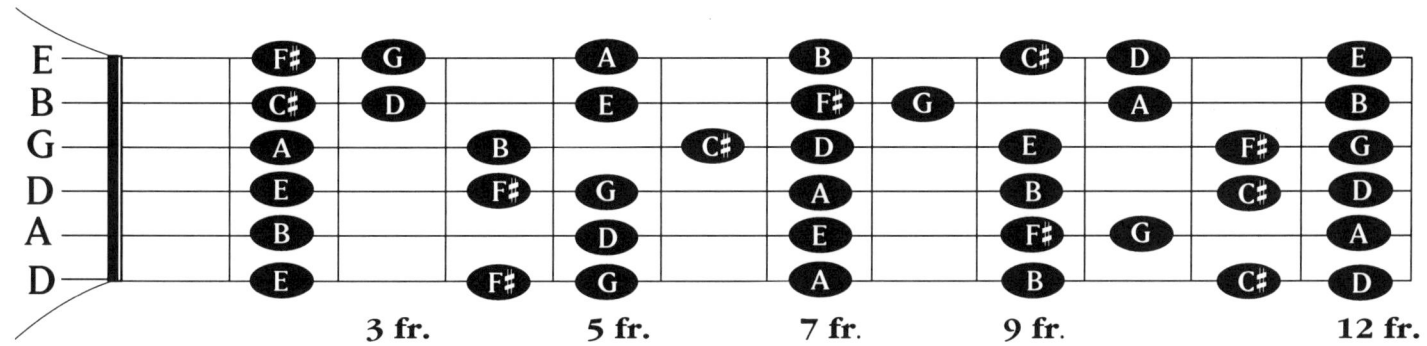

## CHORD DIAGRAMS

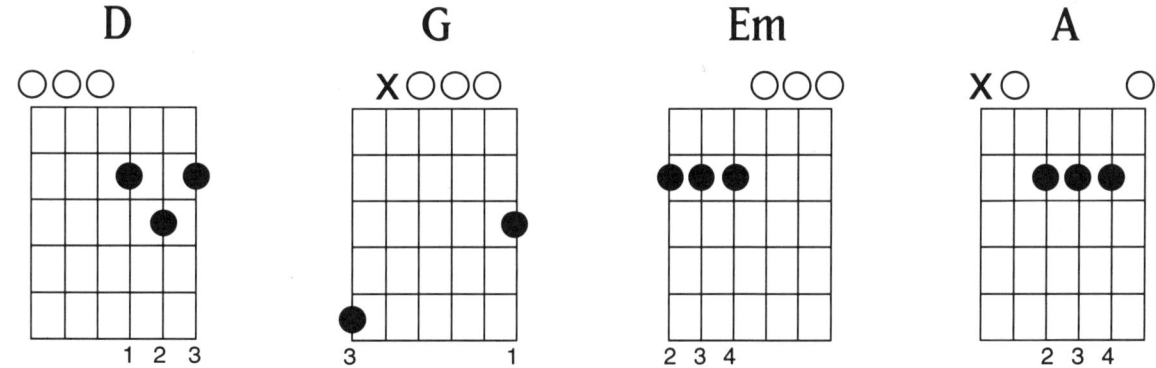

### SEATTLE PSYCHEDELIC #1

This example is in the style of one of Seattle's foremost proponents of alternate tunings, Soundgarden. The arpeggiated chords, with the root and 5th on the lower strings, gives this example a heavy, psychedelic sound that is typical of Soundgarden's songwriting.

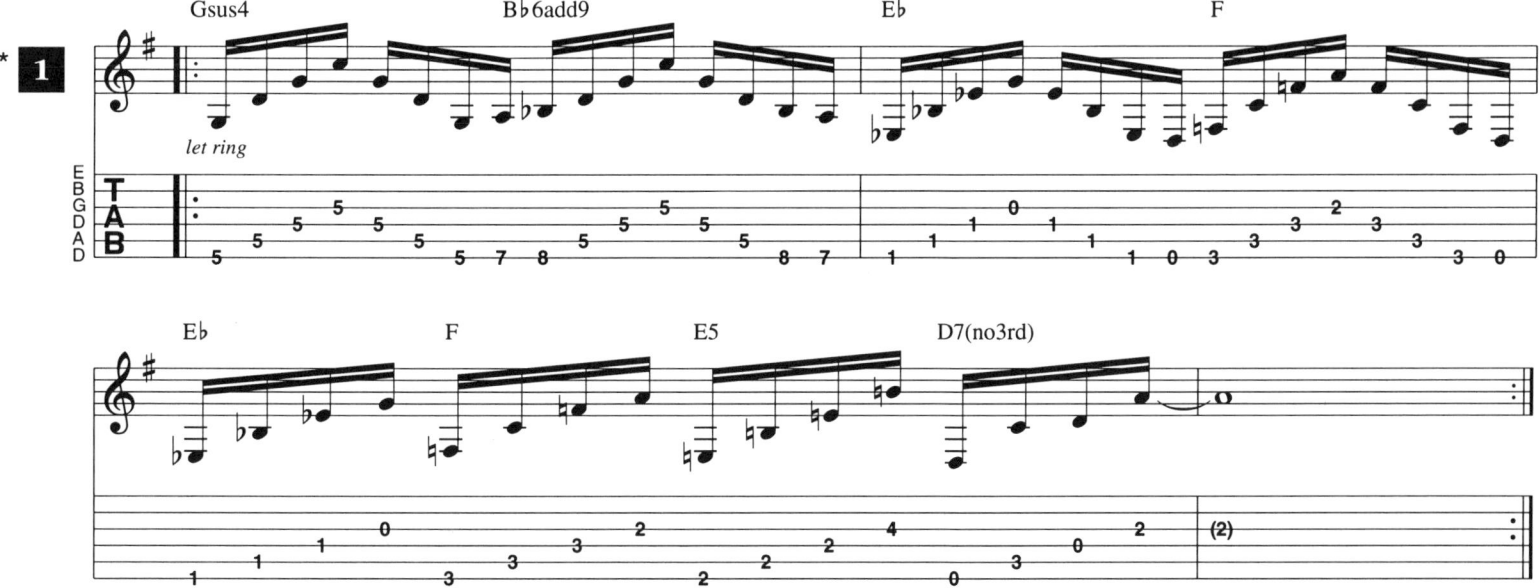

* The numbers in the black boxes correspond with the CD track numbers.

## DROP D IN THE HEART OF TEXAS

Here's another example of how heavy drop D can be, in the style of Texas–based thrashers Pantera. Tuning the 6th string down to D creates a truly powerful sound. Playing 5ths on the lowest two strings generates lots of overtones, and is perfect for distortion. The placement of the power chords in syncopated 16th-note rhythmic patterns is a vital part of the Pantera style.

## "TRAVIS PICKING"

Playing beautiful, arpeggiated triads against a drop-D pedal point is something the Beatles might have done. The fingerpicking style employed here is commonly called "Travis picking," named after Merle Travis, who pioneered the pattern, and can be heard in The Beatles' "Julia" and the Kansas tune "Dust In The Wind." The key to "Travis picking" is to play all of the downstemmed notes with your thumb, and to give the notes on beat 2½ a slight accent.

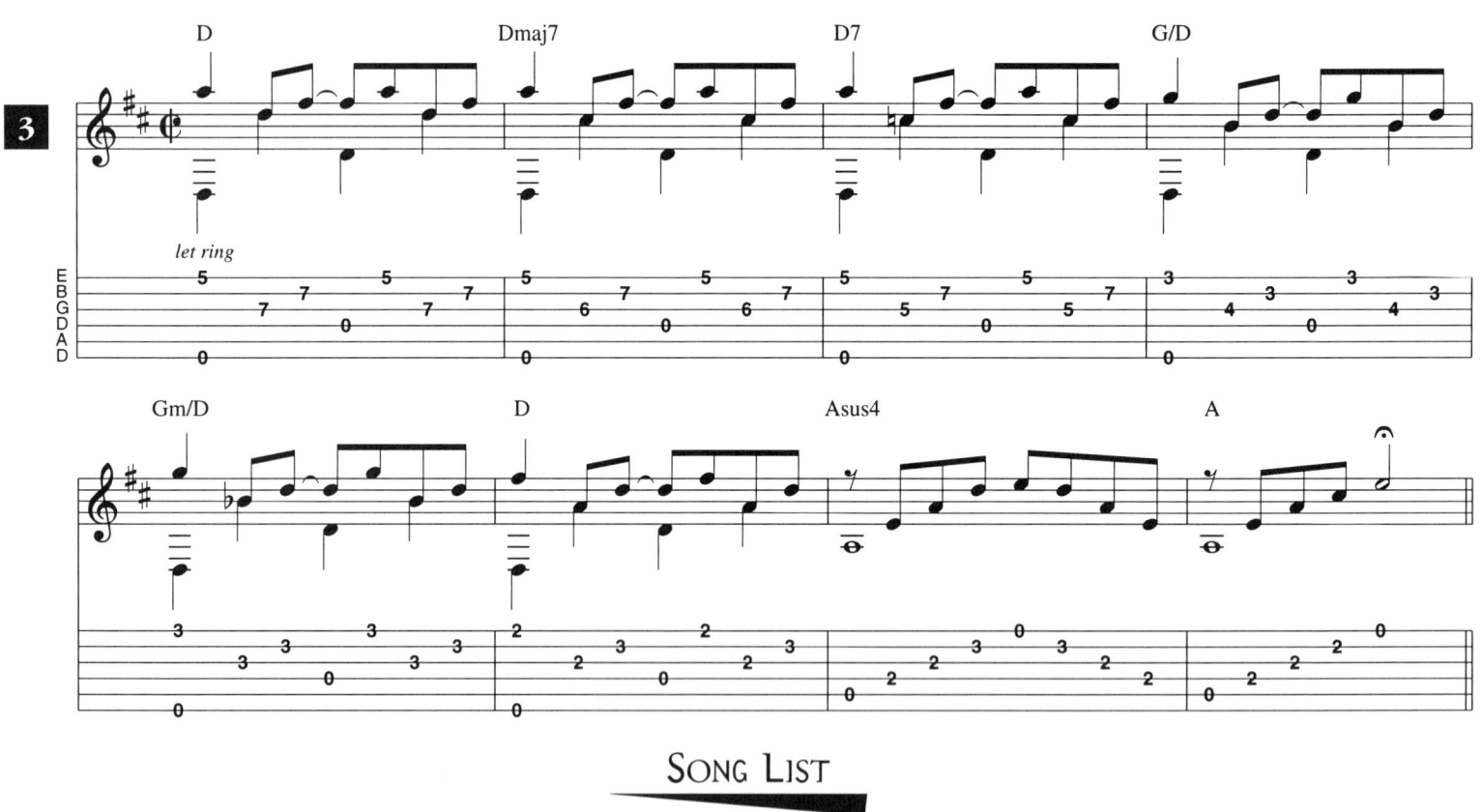

## SONG LIST

**Soundgarden:** "Spoonman," "Let Me Drown," "Black Hole Sun"

**Alice In Chains:** "Them Bones"

**Nirvana:** "Something In The Way" (down a whole step: C G C F A D), "Scentless Apprentice," "Heart Shaped Box" (down a half step: Db Ab Db Gb Bb Eb)

**Rage Against The Machine:** "Killing In The Name," "Take The Power Back," "Freedom," "Wake Up"

**Shawn Colvin:** "Kill The Messenger"

**The Beatles:** "Dear Prudence"

**James Taylor:** "Country Road"

**Leo Kottke:** "Louise," "Mona Ray"

**Van Halen:** "Unchained"

**Joe Satriani:** "Friends," "Midsummer's Daydream"

# DOUBLE DROP D TUNING—D A D G B D

(Tune the 6th and 1st strings down a whole step.)

There are plenty of D's in this tuning, as we twist yet another peg. Now both E strings are tuned down to D, implying the key of D with the bass strings (D A D), and the key of G major (G B D) on the treble strings. This tuning works well in either key, but tends to favor D because of the root on the 6th string.

## D MAJOR SCALE DIAGRAM

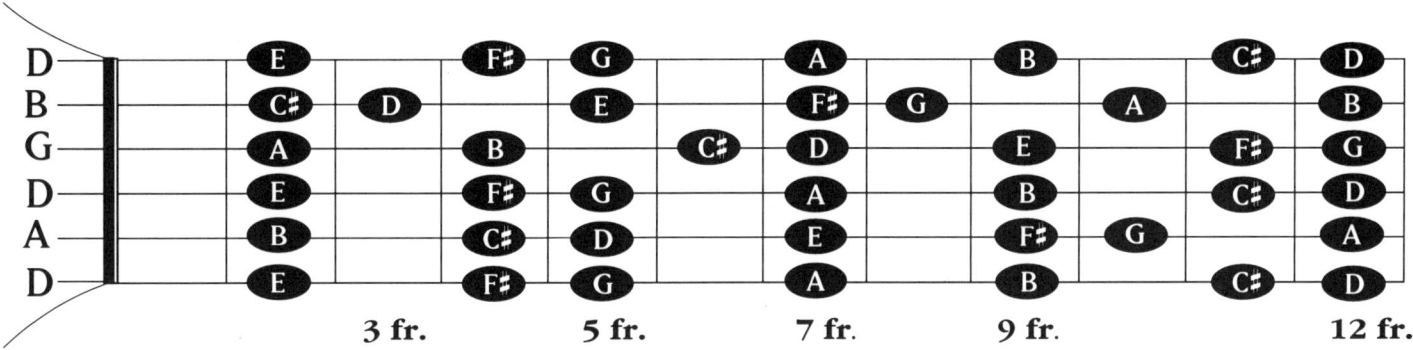

## CHORD DIAGRAMS

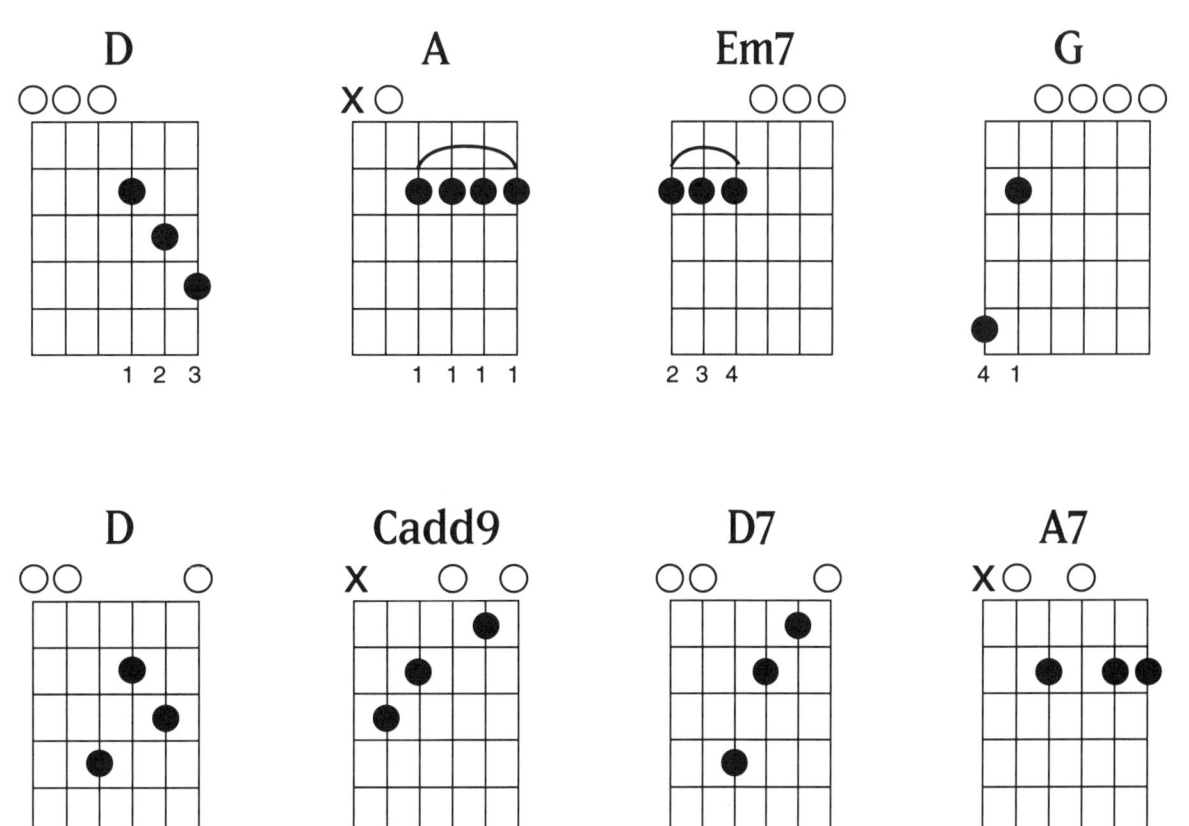

## NASHVILLE NOODLE

This is the way Nashville session ace Ray Flacke might apply this tuning, just pickin' and grinnin' all the way. This style of playing, combining fretted notes with open strings in scalar lines, is taken from banjo players, such as the great Bill Keith, and works particularly well in this tuning.

## ERIC JOHNSON-STYLE BLUES RIFF

Eric Johnson, with his formidable fingerstyle chops, might use double drop D tuning to play something like this. Note the alternating bass, a nod to the "Travis picking" roots of this country blues style. This tuning works wonderfully with the bluesy D pentatonic minor (D F G A C) melody.

### SONG LIST

**Steven Stills:** "Bluebird"
**Eric Johnson:** "Song For George"
**Ray Flacke:** "Long Gone"
**Neil Young:** "Cinnamon Girl"

# OPEN D TUNING—D A D F♯ A D

(Tune the 6th, 2nd and 1st strings down a whole step, and the 3rd string down a half step.)

With this tuning we'll kill two birds with one stone. Open E tuning is essentially the same as open D, because the intervallic relationships between each string are the same in each tuning. Open E is, of course, pitched a whole step higher (E B E G♯ B E). Since the guitar is tuned to an open chord, merely strumming the open strings results in a rich, resonant major chord (either D or E, depending on your tuning). This versatile tuning has long been a favorite of guitarists of all styles, from the Delta blues slide pioneers and transcendental fingerstylists to Seattle grunge rockers. Try moving a standard tuning open E chord form up the neck while strumming all six strings, to discover many sonorous voicings.

## D MAJOR SCALE DIAGRAM

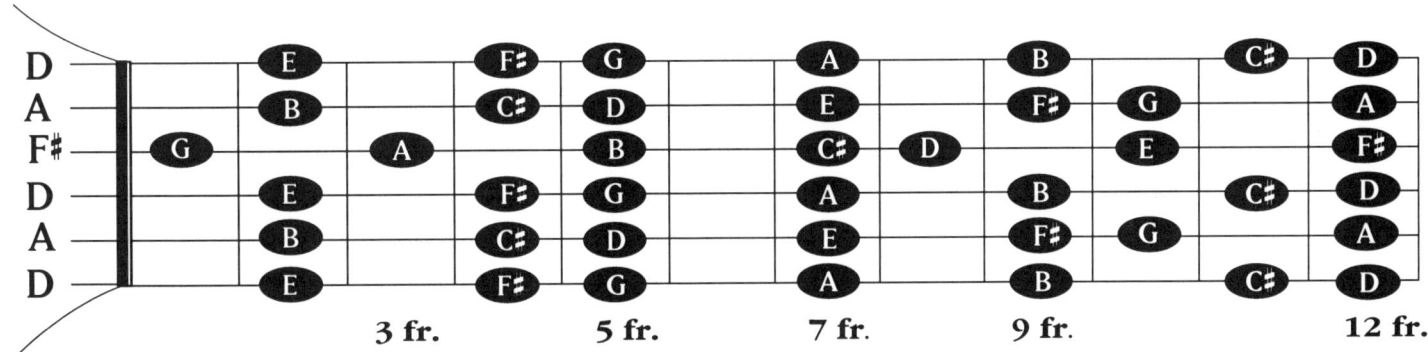

## CHORD DIAGRAMS

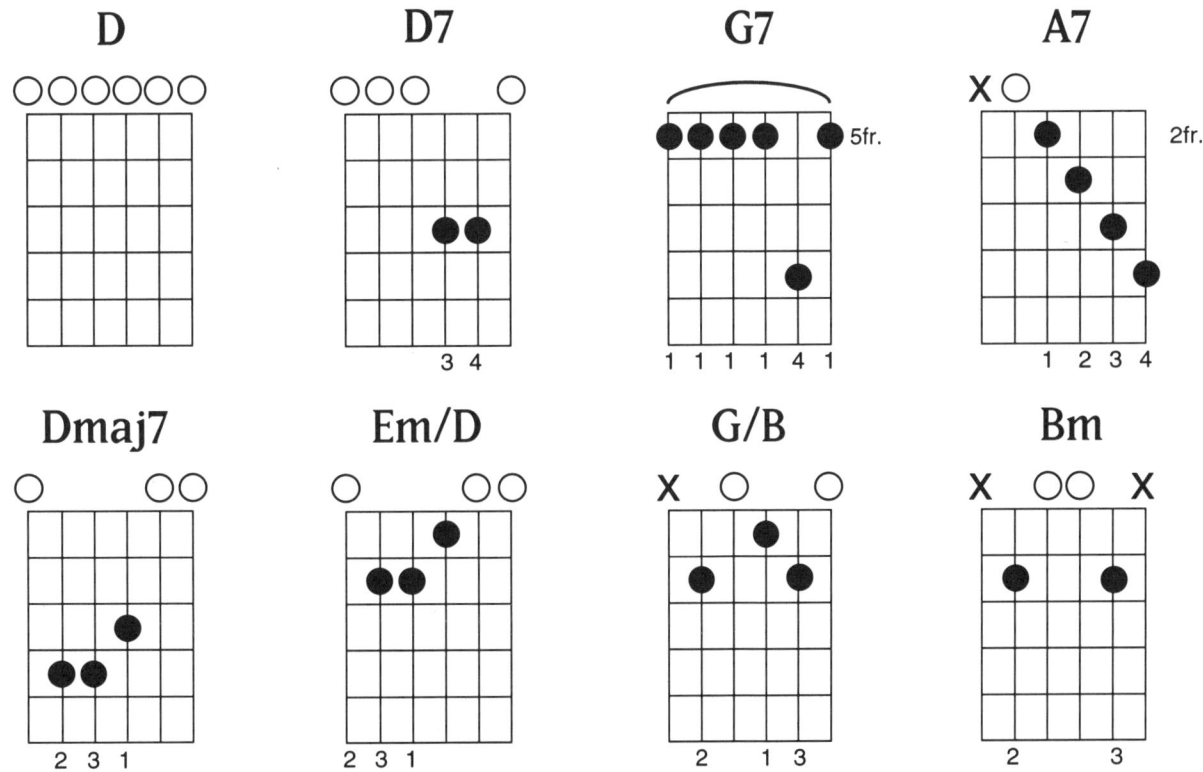

## GRUNGE CHUNK

The use of added 9ths and 4ths lends a mysterious, dark air to the chunky power chords, in this Pearl Jam–inspired example in open D.

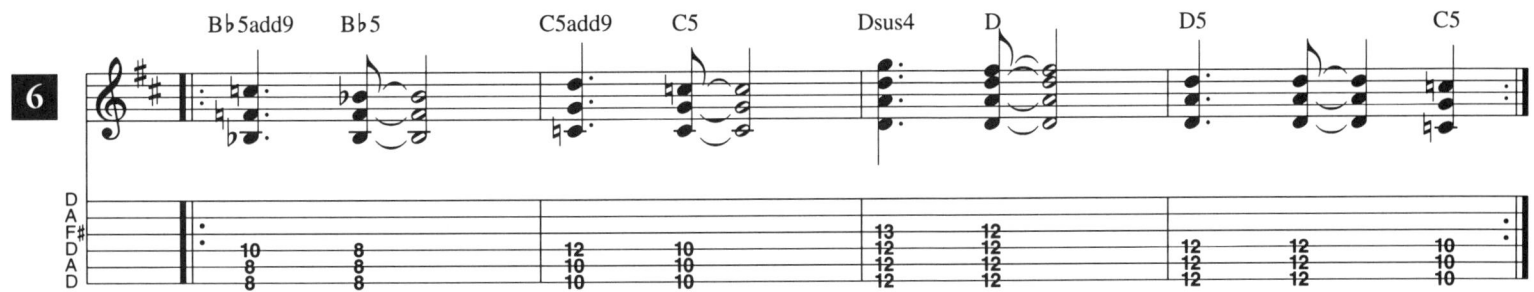

## ADRIAN LEGG-STYLE ELEGANCE

The simple beauty of a melodic line composed almost entirely of chord tones, accompanied by a simple arpeggiated fingerstyle pattern, gives this example an elegant quality, similar to the style of the great English fingerstylist Adrian Legg.

## ELMORE JAMES-STYLE SHUFFLE

D tuning is a wonderful slide tuning, as Robert Johnson and Duane Allman would surely testify (if they could). The blues riff shown here is a classic Elmore James–style slide lick that everyone needs to know.

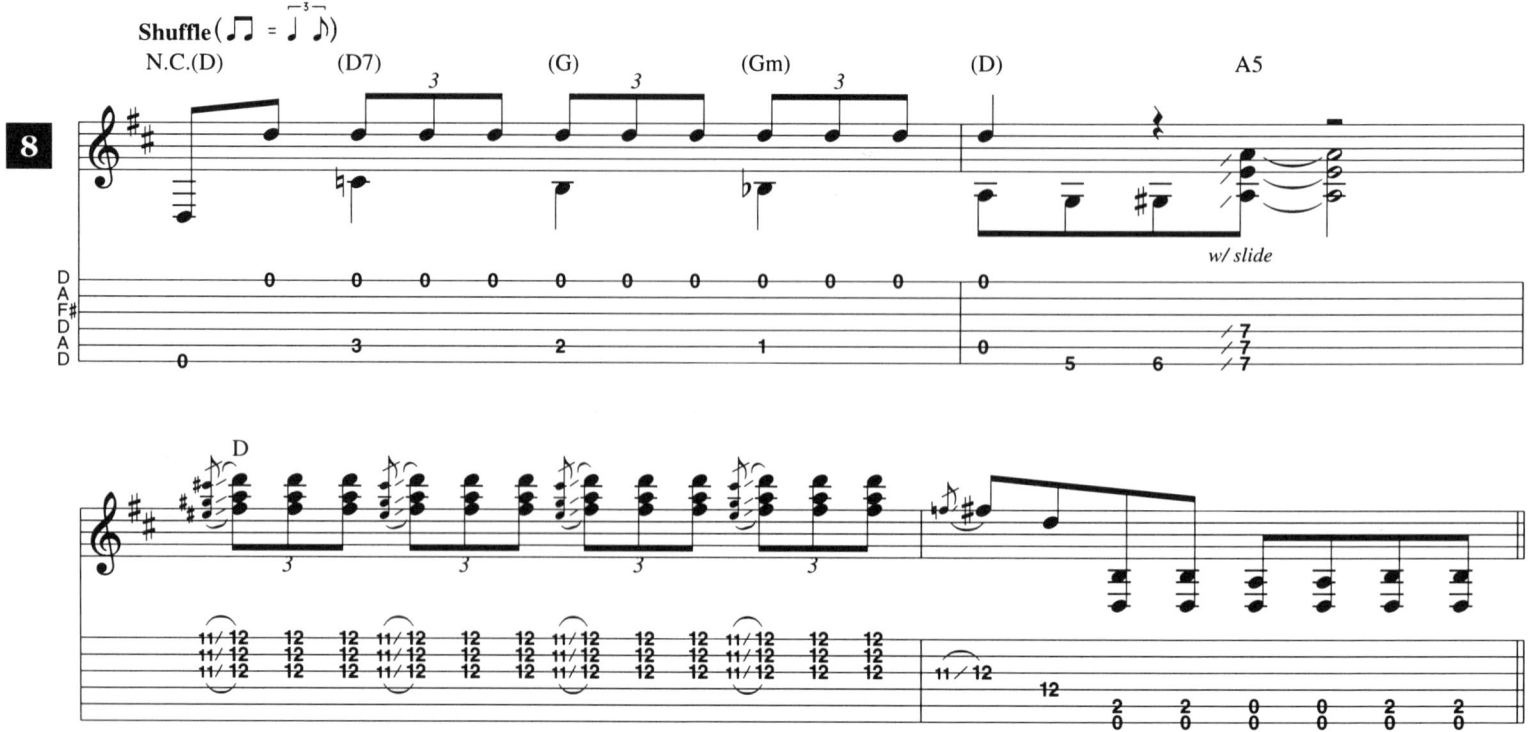

# SONG LIST

**Adrian Legg:** "The Irish Girl"

**Pearl Jam:** "Even Flow"

**Allman Brothers:** "Little Martha" (E)

**Leo Kottke:** "Jesu, Joy Of Man's Desiring"

**Robert Johnson:** "Sweet Home Chicago," "Hellhound On My Trail" (Both E)

**Steve Morse:** "Modoc" (E♭)

**Eric Clapton:** "Blues Before Sunrise," "How Long Blues" (E)

**George Thorogood:** "Madison Blues"

**Joni Mitchell:** "Big Yellow Taxi"

**Black Crowes:** "She Talks To Angels" (E)

**Elmore James:** "Dust My Broom"

# D SUSPENDED (D MODAL) TUNING—D A D G A D

(Tune the 6th, 2nd and 1st strings down a whole step.)

"DADGAD" tuning is a particularly cool tuning because it spells out a Dsus4 chord, thus implying neither major or minor. Long used by the great English and Irish fingerstylists, this tuning has also been embraced by such legendary rock icons as Jimmy Page, and is gaining popularity in the U.S. Try playing a D scale or mode on the G string with all six strings ringing for exotic, Middle Eastern–type sounds. You can also get some very interesting results by playing standard tuning chord forms, such as D or C.

## D MAJOR SCALE DIAGRAM

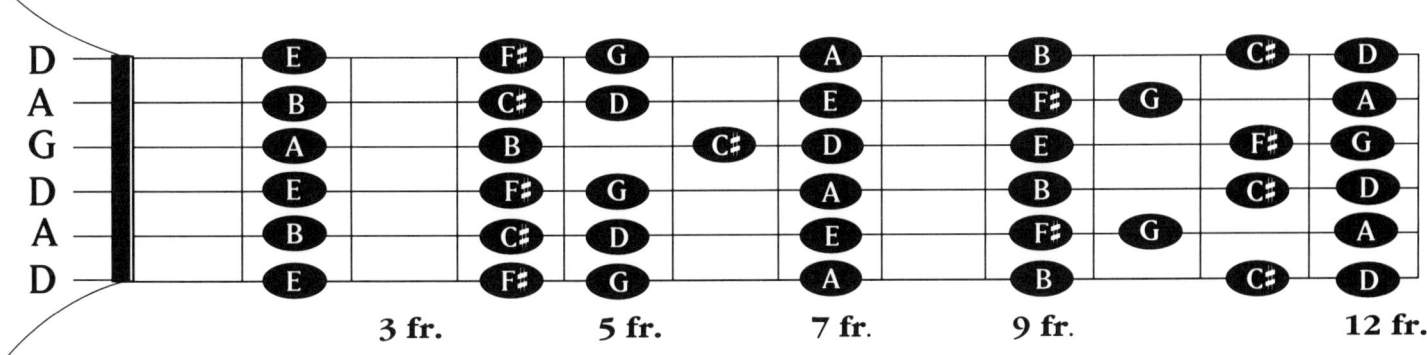

## CHORD DIAGRAMS

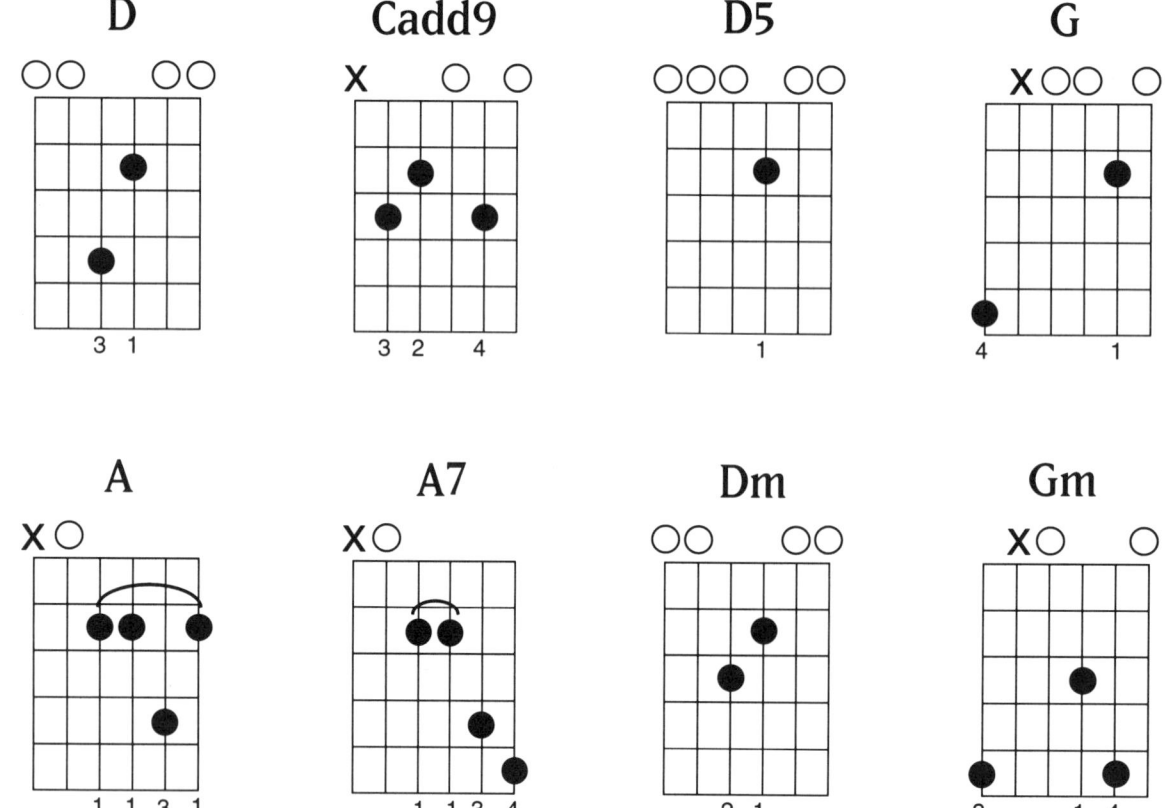

### JIMMY PAGE-STYLE RIFF

Note the movement of the top note over the root and fifth drone. This texture is similar to what is heard in Middle Eastern and Indian musics–both forms of great inspiration to Page, and through him, legions of aspiring guitarists. Jimmy Page, responsible for bringing alternate tunings into the collective consciousness of rock guitarists the world over, might approach this tuning like this:

### BACH'S "JESU, JOY OF MAN'S DESIRING"

French fingerstylist Pierre Bensusan is so enamored of DADGAD tuning that he named his record company after it! This arrangement of Bach's "Jesu, Joy Of Mans Desiring" is in Pierre's lush and beautiful style.

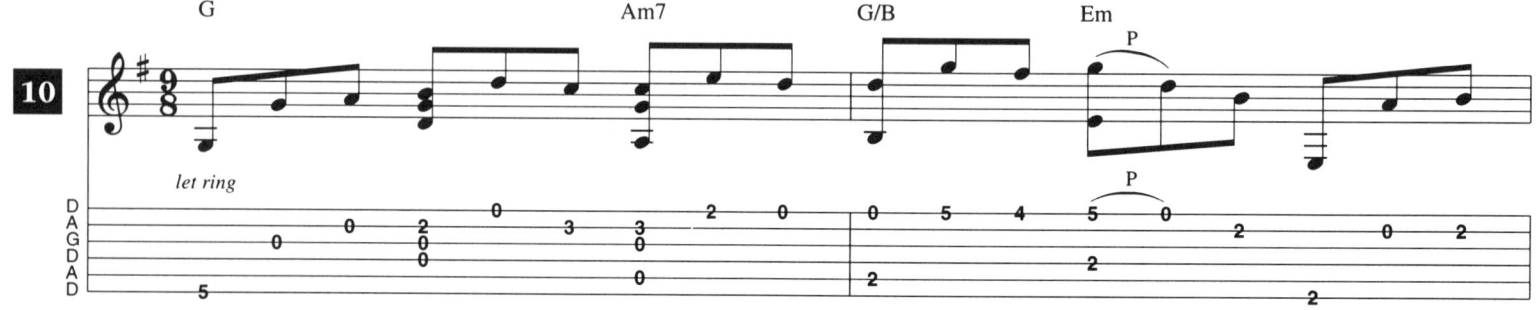

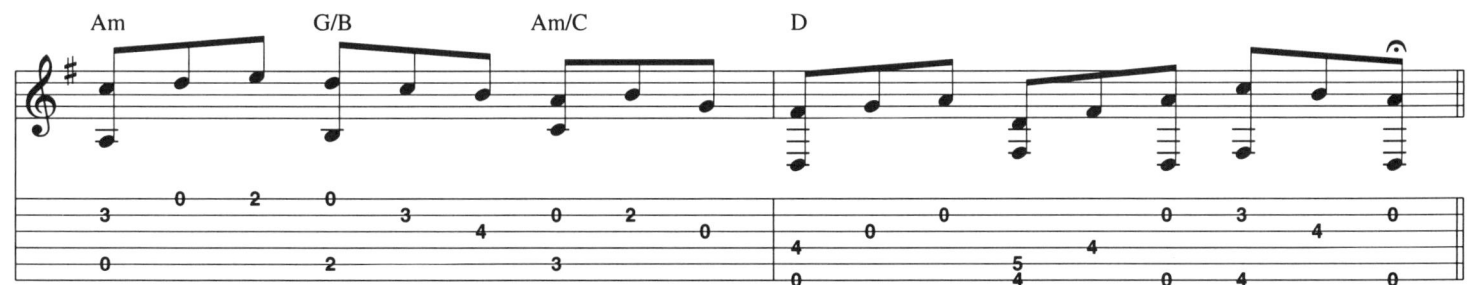

## SONG LIST

**David Wilcox:** "Strong Chemistry," "Farther To Fall"
**Led Zeppelin:** "Kashmir," "Black Mountain Side"
**Cocteau Twins:** "Millemillenary"
**Martin Simpson:** "Go Down Moses"
**Pierre Bensusan:** "Sololai"
**John Renbourn:** "A Maid That's Deep In Love"

# OPEN G TUNING—D G D G B D
(Tune the 6th, 5th and 1st strings down a whole step.)

G tuning is one of the most popular alternate tunings for rock, blues and slide guitar. The intervallic relationships in open A tuning (E A E A C# E) are exactly the same, tuned a whole step higher. Born from the rich earth of the Mississippi Delta, this tuning has been featured on countless recordings. As with all open tunings, a major chord results by barring any fret.

## G MAJOR SCALE DIAGRAM

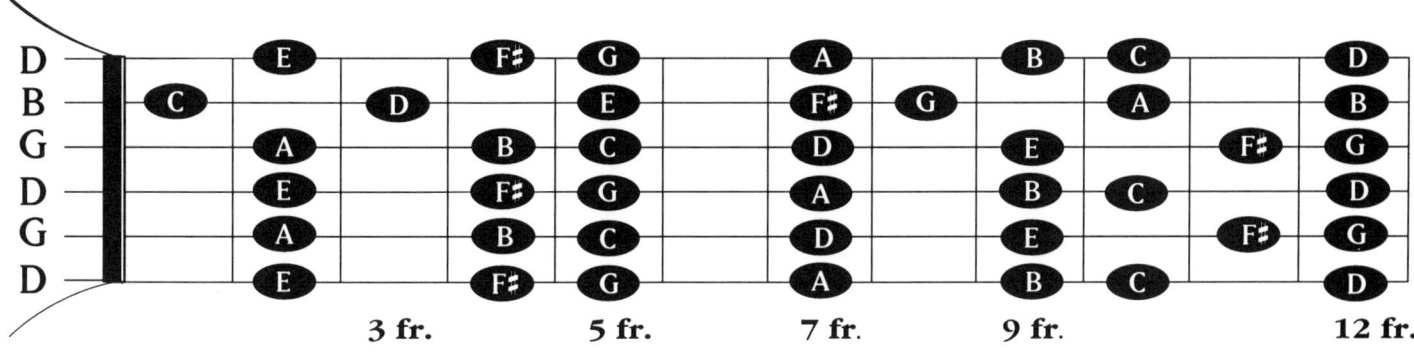

## CHORD DIAGRAMS

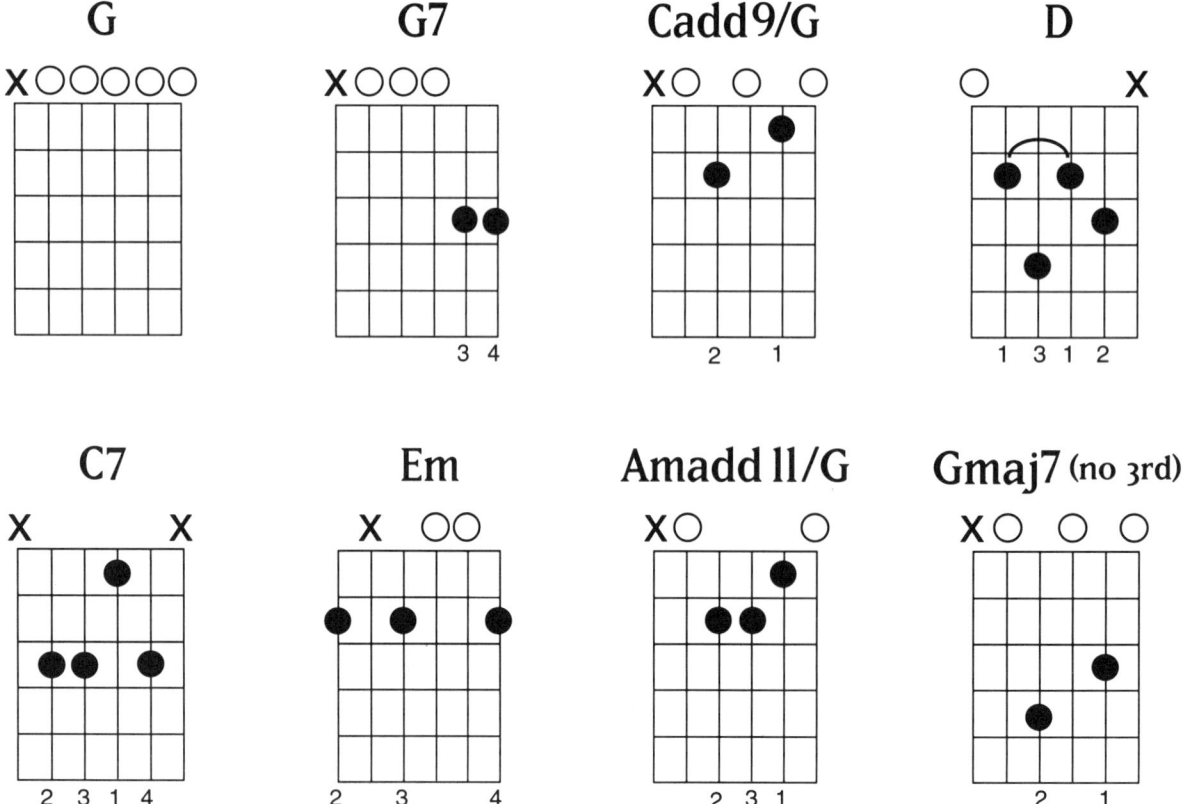

## ROBERT JOHNSON-STYLE LICK

Robert Johnson, the undisputed king of the Delta bluesmen, played some licks like these on some of his classics, such as "Come On In My Kitchen." Better get out the old bottleneck slide for this one! Robert often used a capo on the 2nd fret when playing in this tuning.

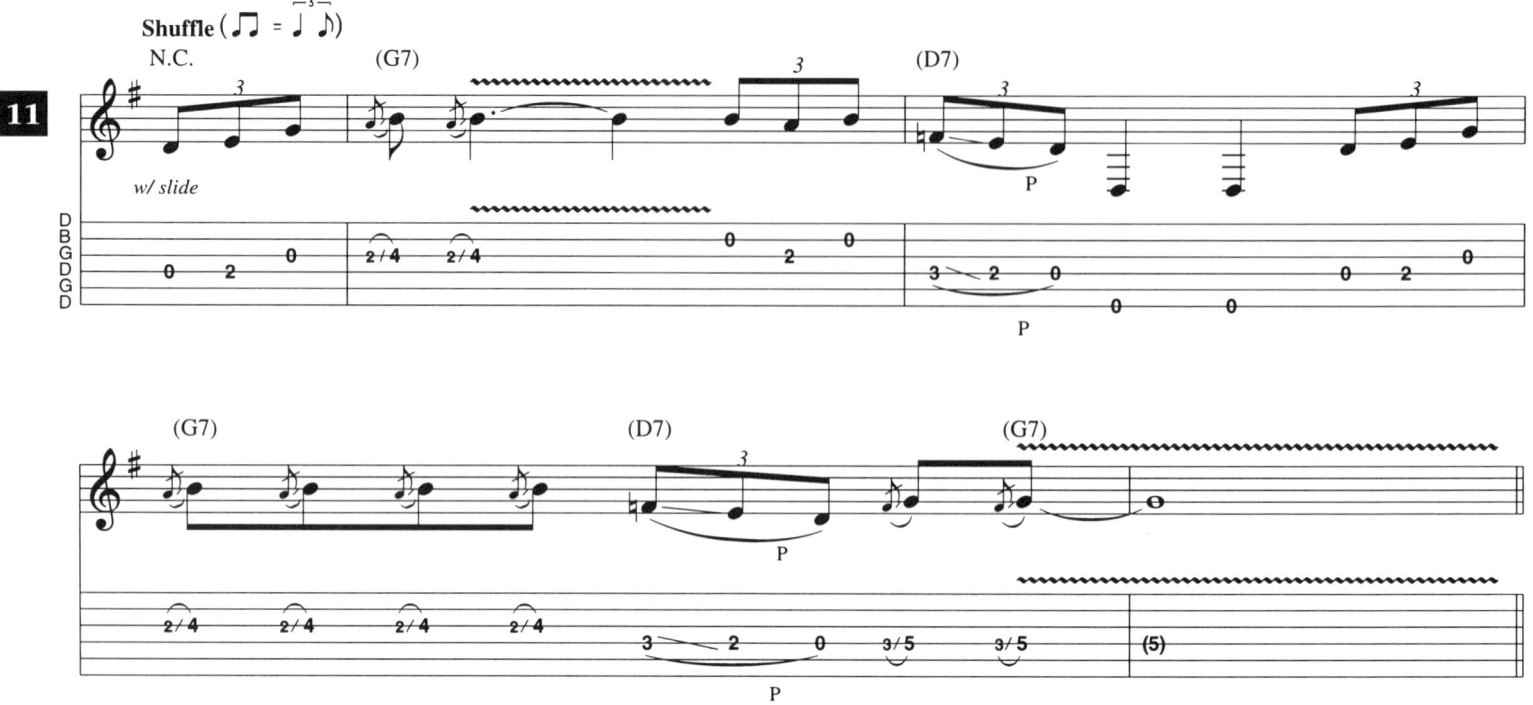

## RY COODER-STYLE VAMP

*Cross Tuning*, a phrase coined by the great Ry Cooder, means playing in a key a 4th or 5th away from the chord to which the guitar is tuned. In this cross-tuned example, the guitar is tuned to open G, but the piece is in D. Instead of the open chord functioning as I, it functions as IV.

## KEITH RICHARDS-STYLE RIFF

You can't have any discussion on G tuning without paying homage to Keith Richards. Many Stones tunes have been written in this tuning. With just a straight barre and a standard tuning minor 7th-chord shape, hundreds of songs have been born. Here's an example in the style of the sinister glimmer twin, one of the living legends of rock guitar.

## SONG LIST

**Rolling Stones:** "Start Me Up," "Brown Sugar," "Honky Tonk Women," "Can't You Hear Me Knockin'," and many more

**Soundgarden:** "Superunknown"

**Stone Temple Pilots:** "Big Empty"

**Robert Johnson:** "Come On In My Kitchen" (A)

**Led Zeppelin:** "Going To California," "In My Time Of Dying" (A), "That's The Way" (G♭)

**Ry Cooder:** "On A Monday," "Little Sister"

**Eric Clapton:** "Motherless Child"

**Shawn Colvin:** "Tenderness On The Block," "Object Of My Affection"

**Bonnie Raitt:** "Thing Called Love" (A)

# OPEN C TUNING—C G C G C E

(Tune the 6th string down two whole steps, the 5th and 4th strings down one
whole step, and the 2nd string up one half step.)

This is a great tuning for playing fingerstyle, as well as crunchy power chords, as the lower strings are tuned way down—loads of C's and G's for powerful 5ths and octaves in the key of C. Try fretting any pair of strings, and move up and down the neck while strumming all six strings for some incredibly resonant chords.

## C MAJOR SCALE DIAGRAM

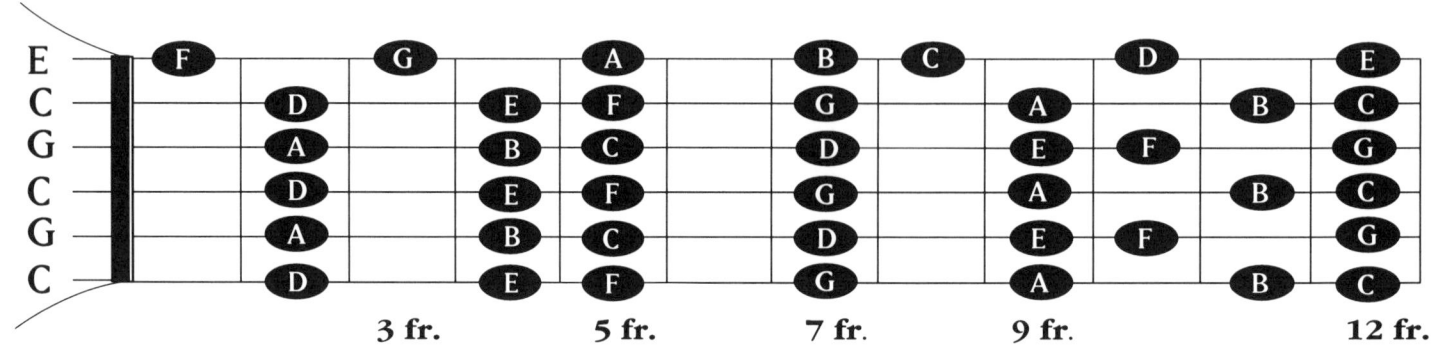

## CHORD DIAGRAMS

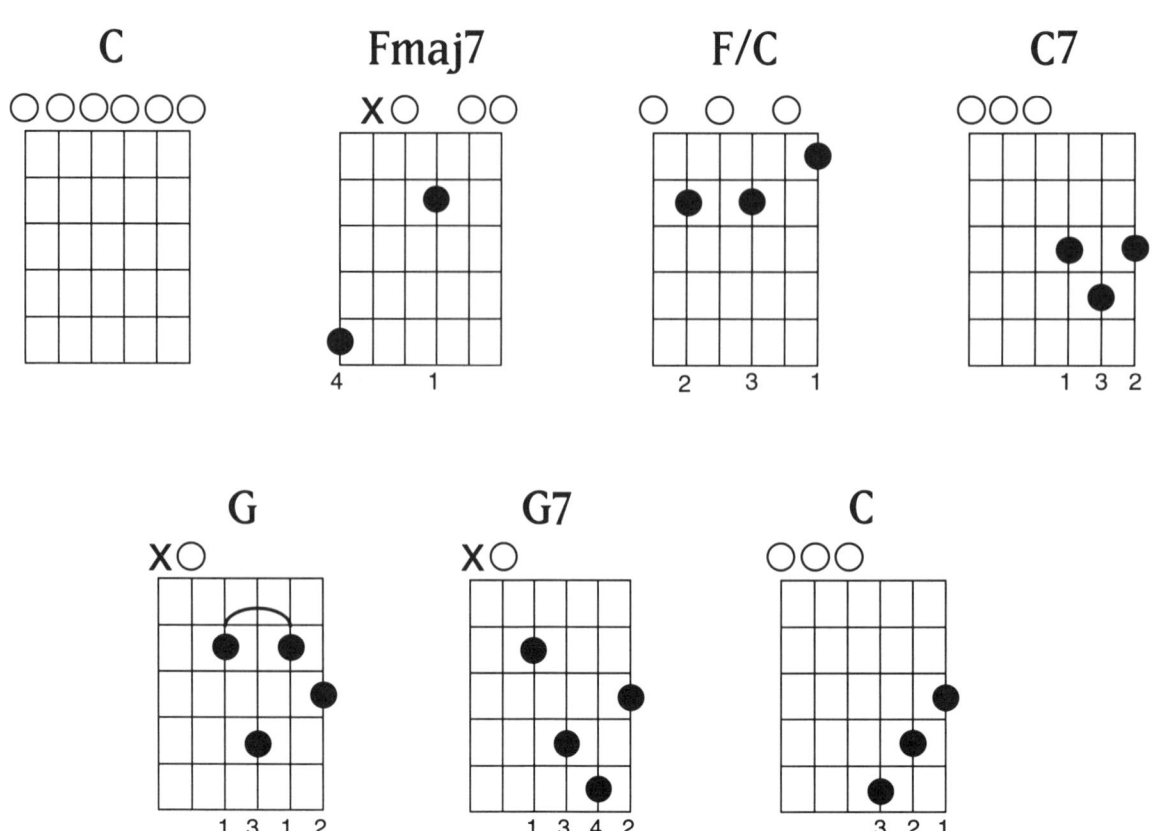

## THICK AND CHUNKY POWER CHORDS

C tuning—it's not always pretty! Crank up your fuzzbox and try this on for size—power chords never sound heavier than when your strings are tuned down a couple of steps!

## SENSITIVE FINGERSTYLE PROGRESSION

Here's a little C tuning, fingerstyle piece for the sensitive singer/songwriter in all of us. An ever-present C pedal point in the bass gives this example a piano-like feel. Notice the poignant Fm (iv in the key of C) in bar 6. Again, "Travis picking" is used for a gentle, folky sound.

# SONG LIST

**David Wilcox:** "New World," "Show The Way," "Eye Of The Hurricane"

**Led Zeppelin:** "Hats Off To (Roy) Harper"

**William Ackerman:** "Townsend Shuffle"

# G6TH TUNING—D G D G B E

(Tune the 6th and 5th strings down a whole step.)

G6 is the first cousin of open G tuning. This tuning allows you the luxury of playing many of the licks and chords you already know in the key of G major or minor (at least those that lie on the top four strings), while keeping the 1 and 5 of the key in the low strings.

## G MAJOR SCALE DIAGRAM

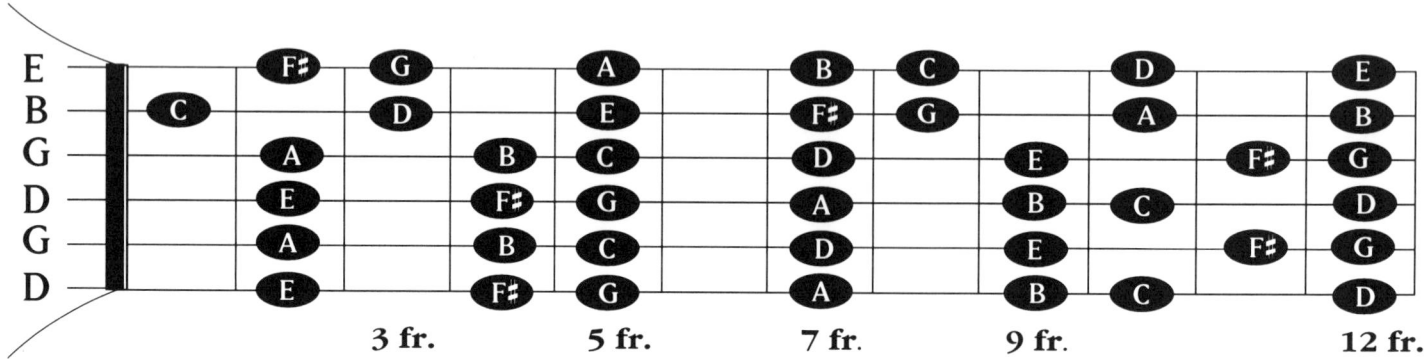

## CHORD DIAGRAMS

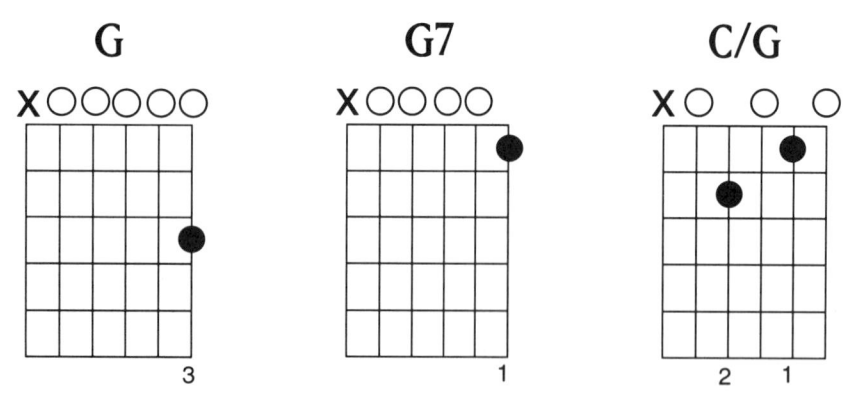

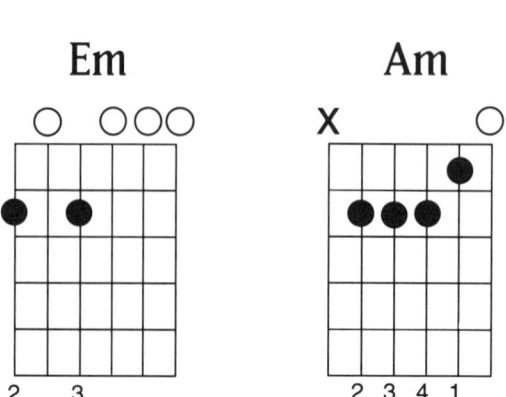

## SEATTLE PSYCHEDELIC #2

The use of fretted notes ringing against open strings a whole or half step away gives this example a swirling, psychedelic sound typical of Soundgarden.

## CHICKEN PICKIN' LICK

Adrian Legg has always been influenced by American country music. This tuning, having the root on the 5th string (G), and the fifth on the 6th string (D), allows for an alternating bass. The standard tuning of the rest of the guitar enables Adrian to flex his prodigious chicken pickin' chops. Here's an example of how he might approach this tuning.

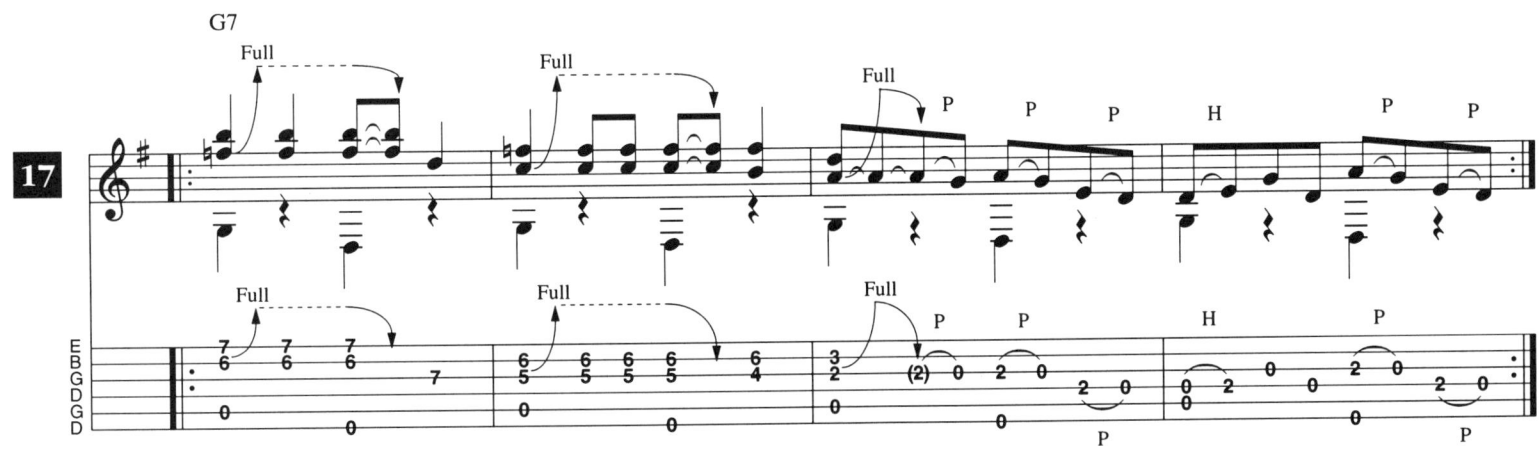

## SONG LIST

**Soundgarden:** "Superunknown," "Fresh Tendrils"
**Adrian Legg:** "Chicken Little's Last Stand"
**Chet Atkins:** "Yellow Bird"

# C6 TUNING—C A C G C E

(Tune the 6th string down two whole steps, the 4th string down a whole step, and the 2nd string up a half step.)

## C MAJOR SCALE DIAGRAM

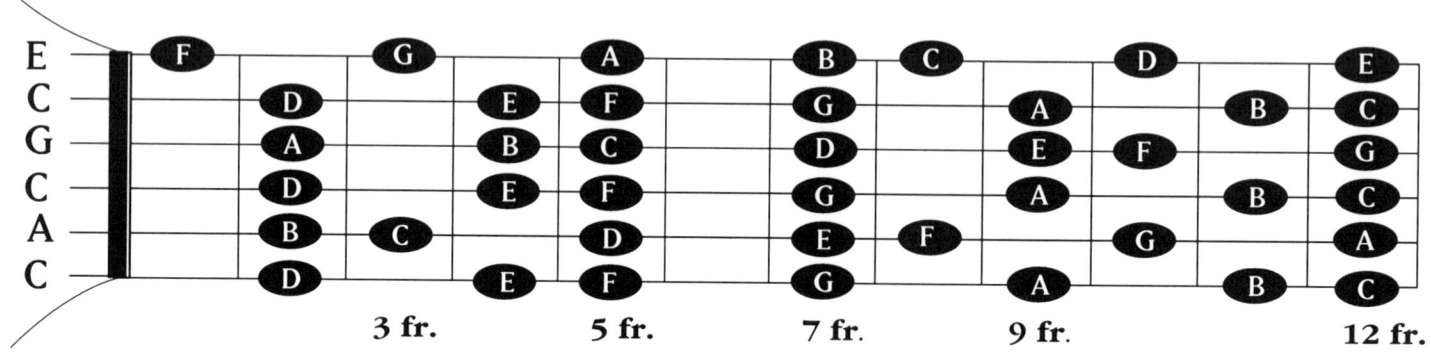

## CHORD DIAGRAMS

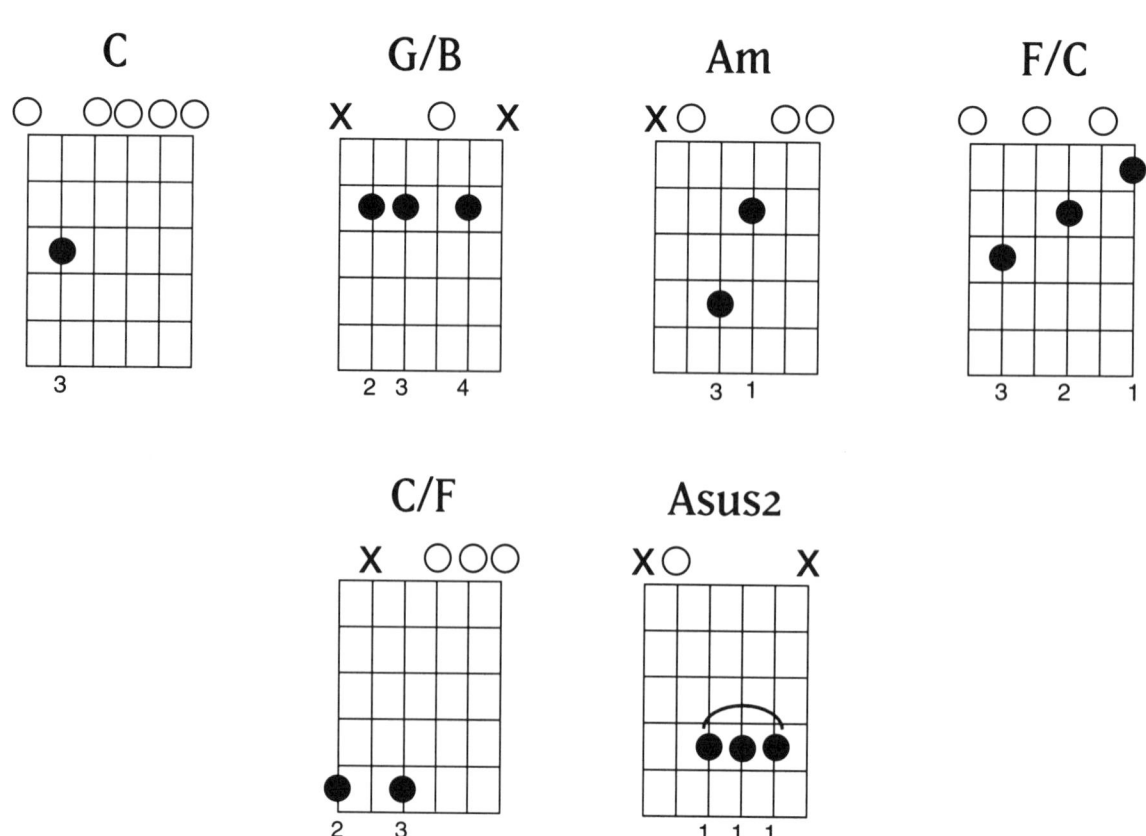

## JIMMY PAGE-STYLE PROGRESSION

Jimmy Page was greatly influenced by Bert Jansch and other English acoustic guitarists, as the harmonies and fingerpicking of this Page-inspired example will attest. A simple I-V progression takes on a whole new life in this deep, resonant tuning. Page has expressed a preference for alternate tunings that are not open (major chord) tunings, such as this one, once declaring that he "can get more chords out of them."

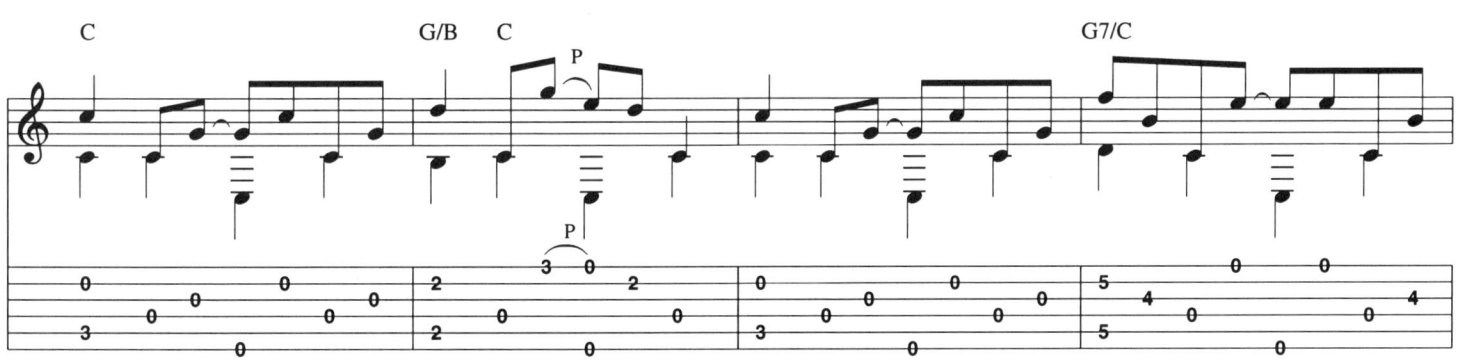

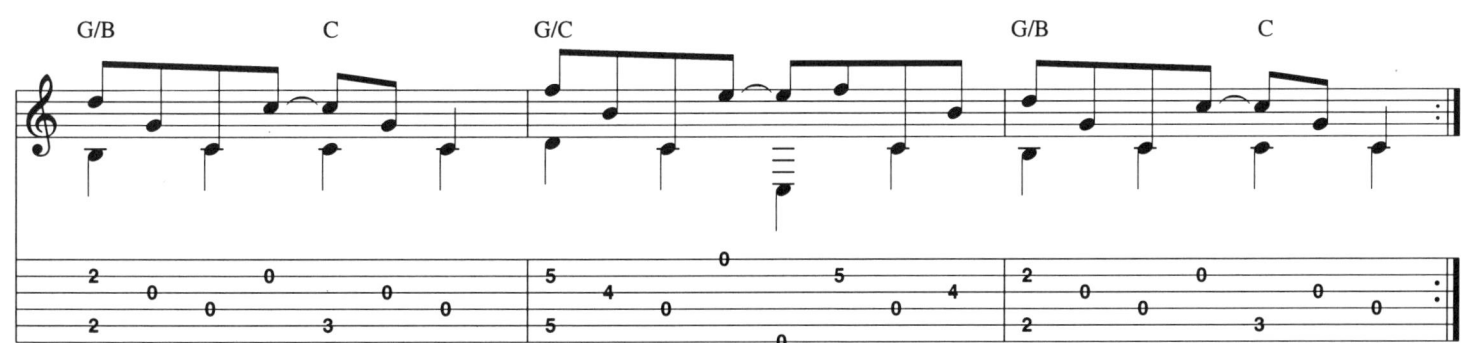

## SONG LIST

**Led Zepppelin:** "Bron-Yr-Aur," "Friends"

# C MAUNA LOA (C6TH) TUNING—C G C G A E

(Tune the 6th string down two whole steps, and the 5th, 4th and 2nd strings down a whole step.)

This tuning is attributed to the traditional Hawaiian guitar style called *slack key*. (A more detailed discussion of slack key tunings occurs on page 29.) This tuning forms a C6 chord (C E G A) in an open voicing. This tuning is also used by lap steel players for Western swing.

## C MAJOR SCALE DIAGRAM

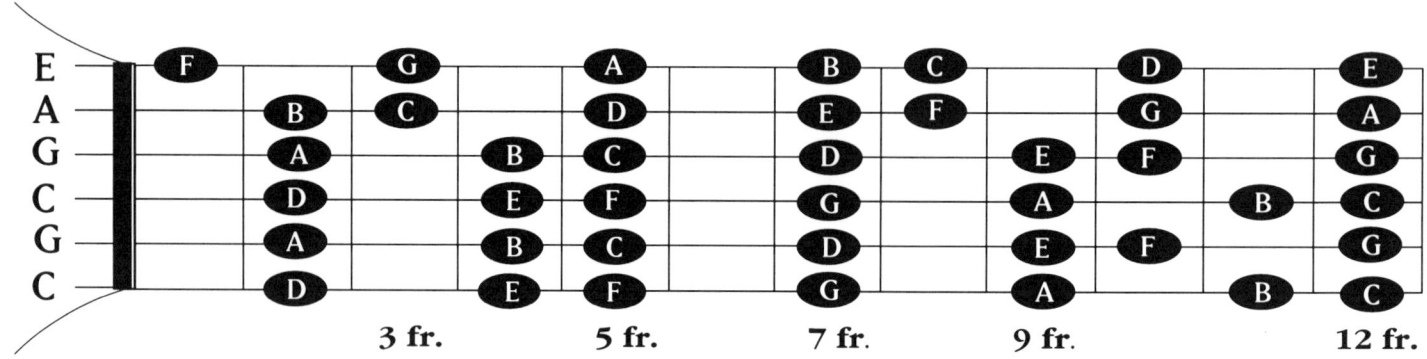

## CHORD DIAGRAMS

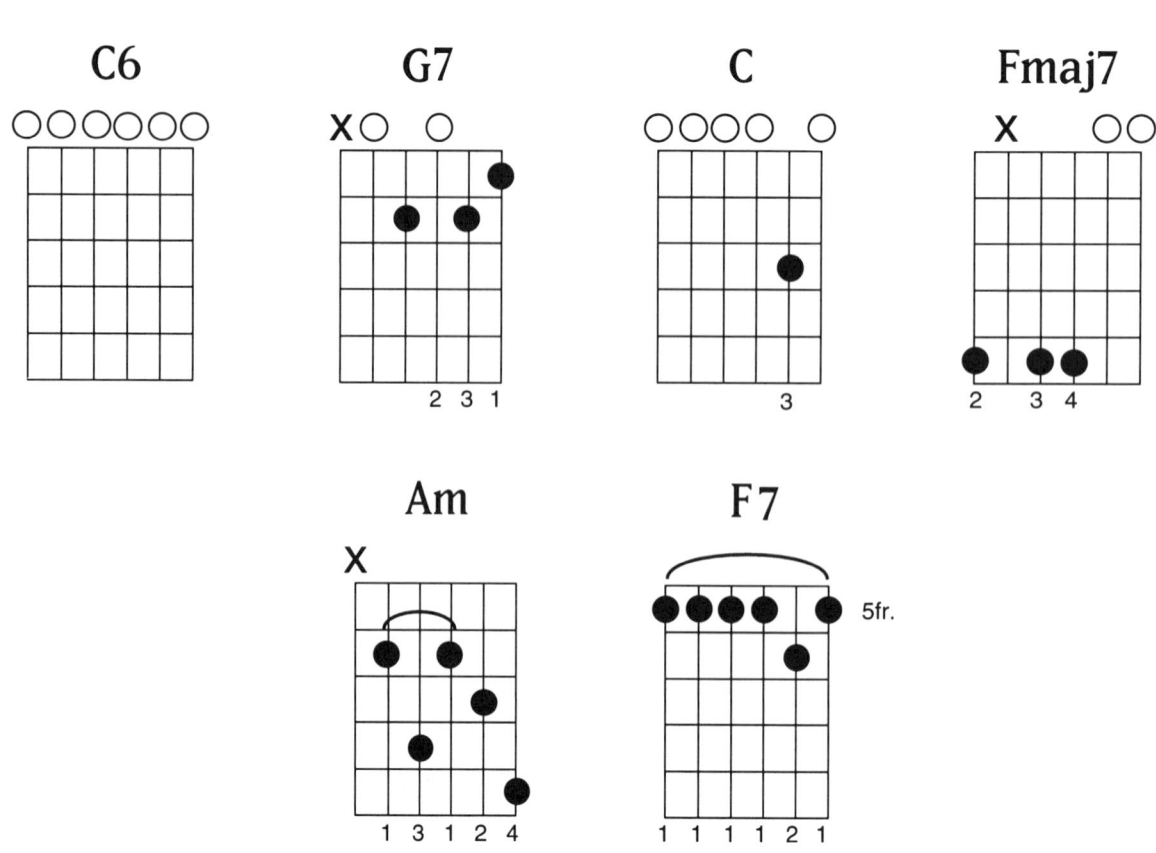

## HAWAIIAN-STYLE CHORDS

Here's an example guaranteed to make you long for those swaying palms and gentle ocean breezes. The use of passing chords (bar 1, beat 4) and neighbor chords (bar 2, beat 4) is typical in Hawaiian music.

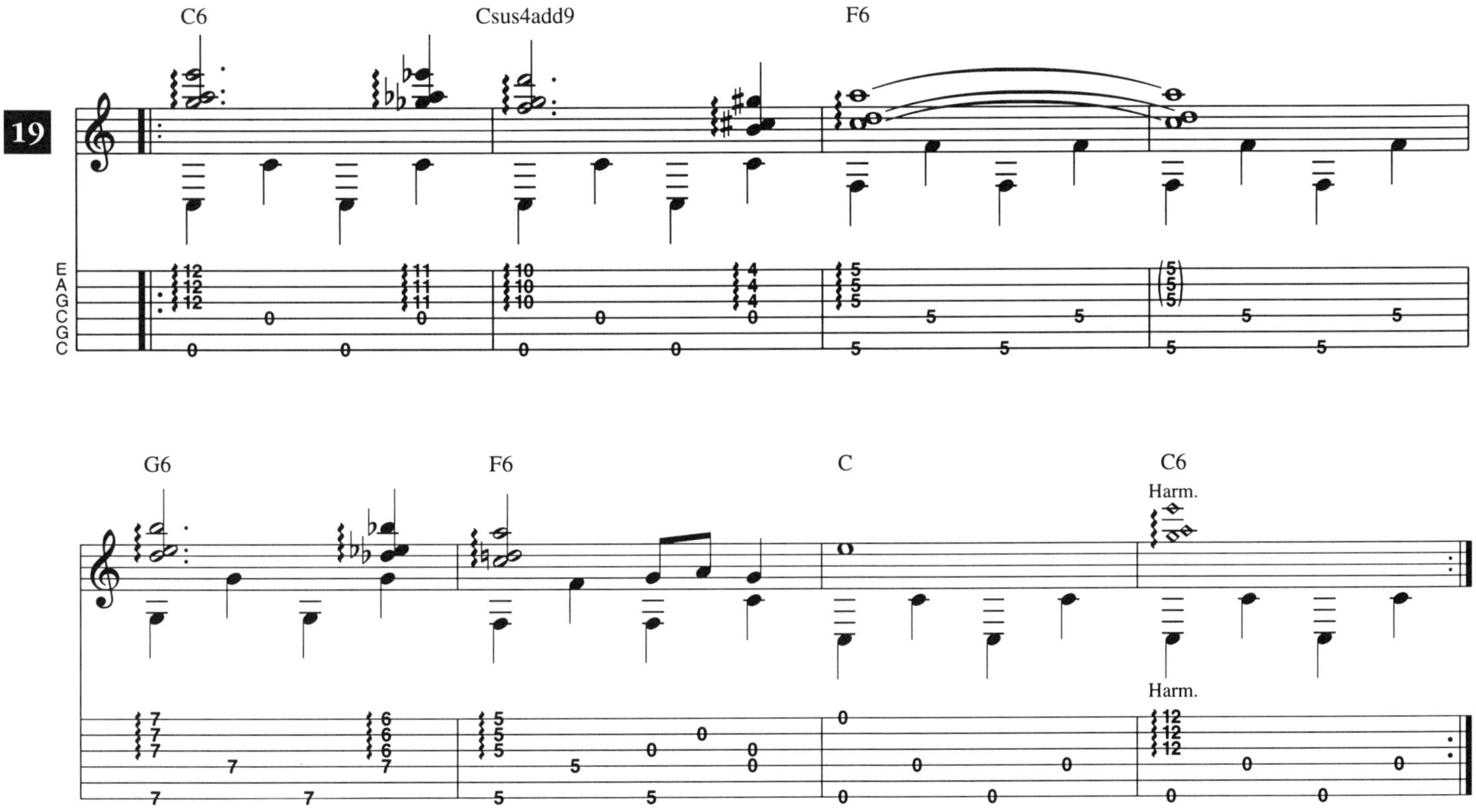

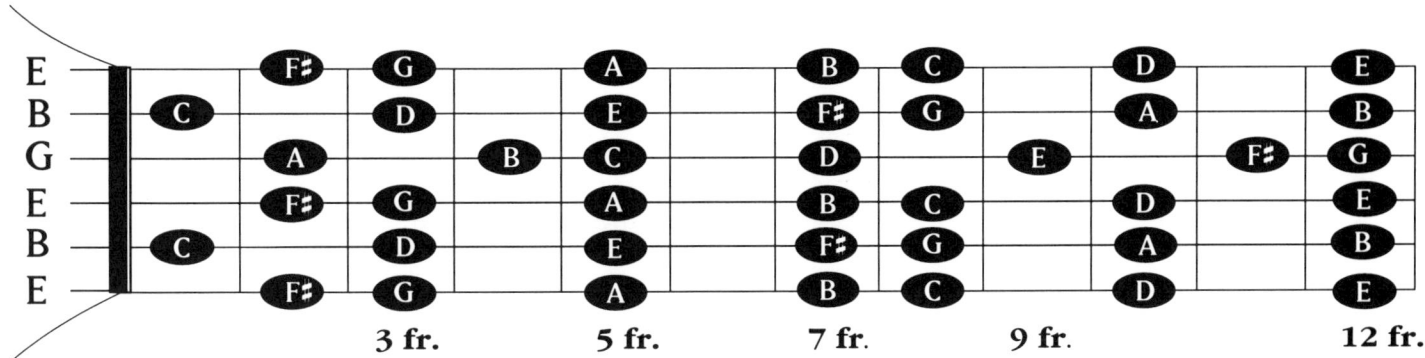

# E MINOR TUNING—E B E G B E

(Tune the 5th and 4th strings up a whole step.)

The bluesman Skip James used E minor tuning almost exclusively, and the late great blues guitarist Albert Collins was noted for his playing in F minor tuning (E minor tuning, up a half step). Since the guitar is tuned to an E minor chord, think sad and bluesy. This tuning is great for slide playing in minor keys.

## E MINOR SCALE DIAGRAM

## CHORD DIAGRAMS

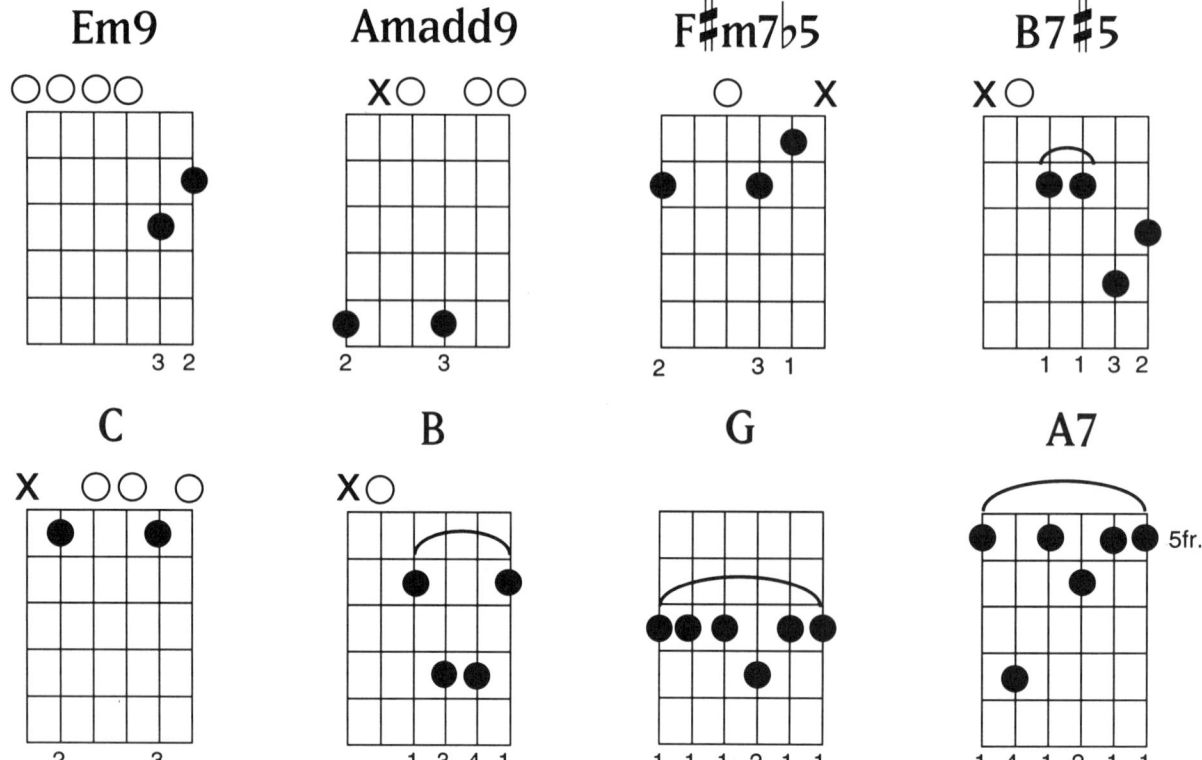

## SWAMPY E MINOR BLUES

The root and 5th hold down the bass strings, while the treble strings remain in standard tuning—perfect for playing swampy E pentatonic minor blues licks like the ones in this example. The C (VI) and B (V) chords, often used in minor blues, come from the E harmonic minor scale (E F♯ G A B C D♯). Think "St. James Infirmary" or "The Thrill Is Gone."

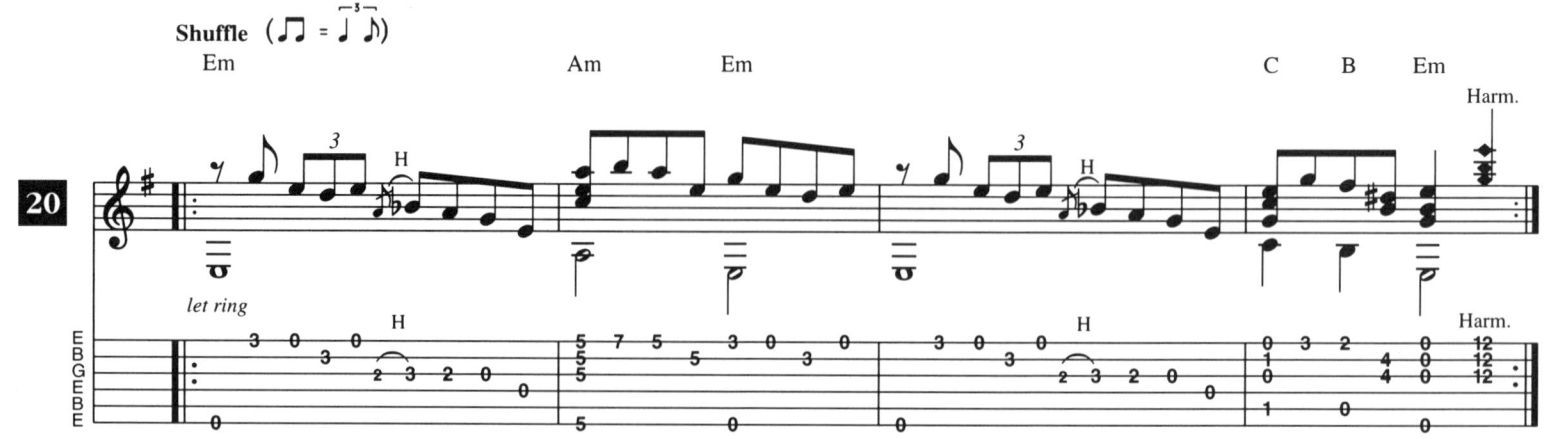

## SONG LIST

**Skip James:** "Hard Time Killin' Floor"
**R.E.M.:** "Monty Got A Raw Deal"
**Albert Collins:** "Iceman" (Fm)

# C G D G B E TUNING

(Tune the 6th string down two whole steps, and the 5th string down a whole step.)

Think of this tuning as your chance to play everything you already know on the treble strings, while having the ability to play chunky 5ths or beautiful lines on the bass strings. Especially nice for the key of C, this one can be as light as a feather or crushingly heavy.

## C MAJOR SCALE DIAGRAM

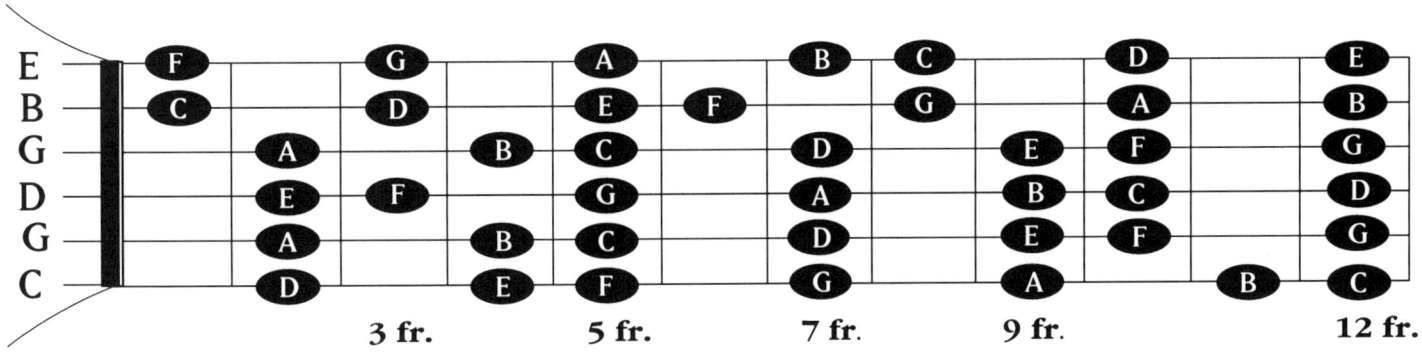

## CHORD DIAGRAMS

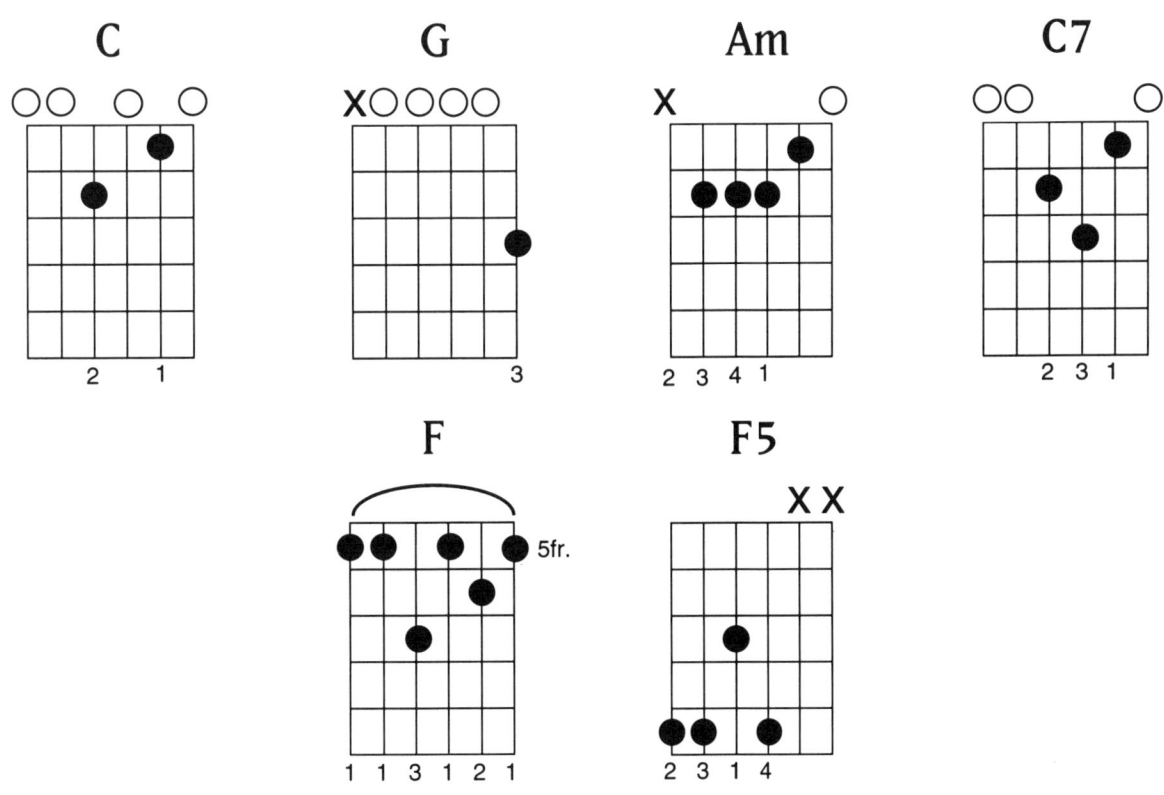

## SOUNDGARDEN-STYLE RIFF

This heavy example in 12/8 exhibits some smooth voice leading between the chords, à la Soundgarden.

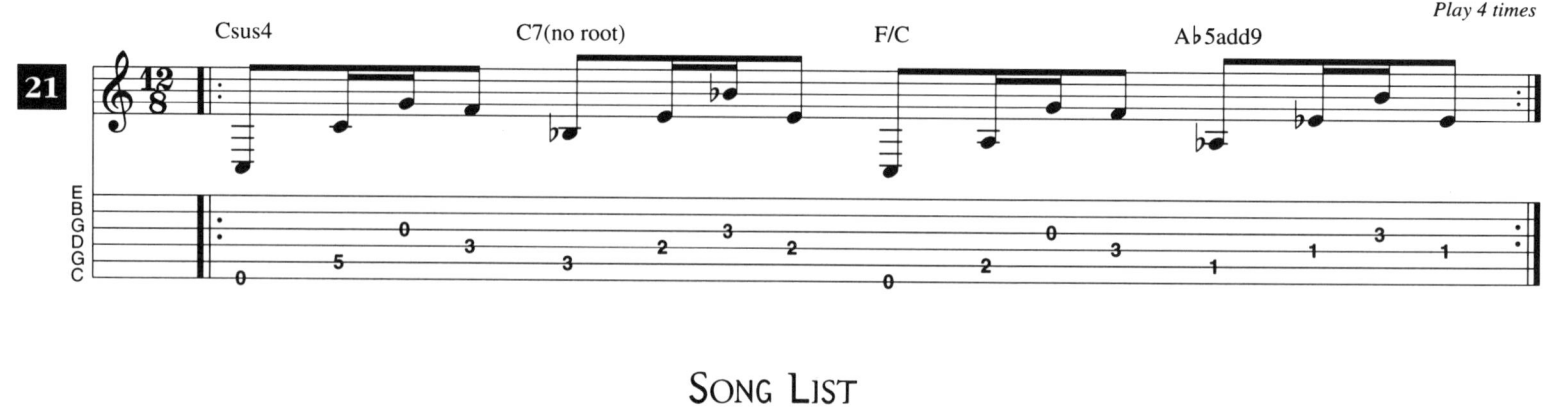

## SONG LIST

**Soundgarden:** "Limo Wreck," "Mailman"
**Lindsey Buckingham:** "Never Going Back Again"
**Christopher Parkening:** "Sheep May Safely Graze" (J.S.Bach)

# ALTERED STATES

Welcome to the outer-reaches of the alternate tuning universe, where there are no limits on your imagination. The tunings in this section are really bizarre, and most are seldom used in more than one song. These examples show what you can achieve by cranking and cranking tuners until you are happy with the results. To start off, let's take a look at the incredibly creative musicians of Sonic Youth.

Traveling with as many as 25 guitars, each tuned for specific songs, no band can touch these guys for sheer tuning terror. (The tunings and string gauges are written on tape on the back of each headstock, and there are no strings lighter than a .017.) Many of their tunings exhibit unison and half-step intervals between strings; some tunings even forego the normal low to high string order! As you might imagine, trying to figure out a Sonic Youth song without knowing the tuning in advance is like bailing out the Mississippi River with a spaghetti strainer. Using extended techniques, including playing with a screwdriver, rubbing feedback-laden screaming guitars against each other, and displaying an obvious disregard for convention, Sonic Youth has initiated countless musicians into the outer limits of alternate tunings. The wonderful part of all of this is that once you know the tunings, actually playing the song doesn't require any amazing guitar pyrotechnics!

On the Sonic Youth album *Experimental Jet Set, Trash And No Star*, Lee Ranaldo favors G G C G C D, G G B D G A and C# F# C# F# A# B. Kim Gordon (bass) played guitar on "Skink" and "Bone" in B E D D B B tuning. Try this one on for size: On the song "Sweet Shine" Thurston Moore plays in E G D G E D (the 2nd string lower than the 3rd), while Ranaldo plays in E E B B E F#.

## E G D G E D TUNING

This example, in E G D G E D tuning, is in the style of "Dirty Boots" from Sonic Youth's album *Goo*. The 2nd string is tuned down to E, making it sound lower than the 3rd string. (It might be a good idea to put an extra heavy string on, especially if your B string is on the lighter side.) The 3rd and 2nd strings (G and E) set a droning backdrop for the melodic line, which is played on the 1st and 4th strings. This use of moving octaves against open strings is a hallmark of Sonic Youth's signature sound. "No chord" (N.C.) appears in the notation because the musical texture of this example stems from the relationship of the melodic line to the drone, rather than from a certain series of chords in a progression. In a certain way, this example has more in common with Eastern music (whose texture is most often composed of melody, drone and rhythm) than with the harmonic, chord-based music of the Western world. (The same can be said of the forthcoming examples, 23 and 24.) The pitches used in this example are from the E Aeolian mode (E F♯ G A B C D).

## E G♯ E G♯ E G♯ TUNING

Here's an example in the tuning from "Expressway To Yr. Skull," E G♯ E G♯ E G♯, consisting of pairs of major 3rds in the key of E major. (The 1st and 2nd strings are tuned down to match the 3rd and 4th strings exactly.) Again, you may want to replace the top two strings with heavier gauges if the sound is too "floppy." Playing the melody on the three G♯ strings, combined with the three open E strings droning, creates a full, rich sound in this example. Again, "no chord" appears in the music, due to the melody/drone texture. The pitches used in this example are from the E major scale (E F♯ G♯ A B C♯ D♯).

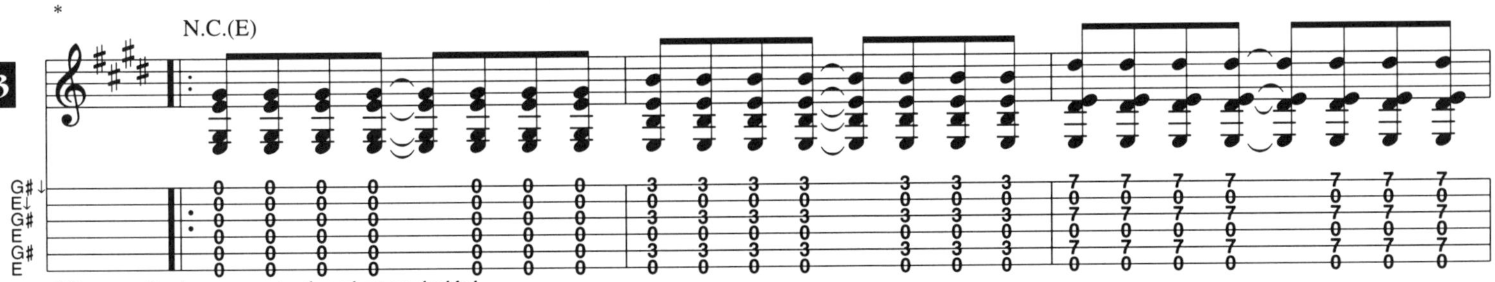

\* Because of tuning, many notes throughout are doubled.
For ease of reading, these notes are only shown once in notation.
All notes actually played are shown in TAB.

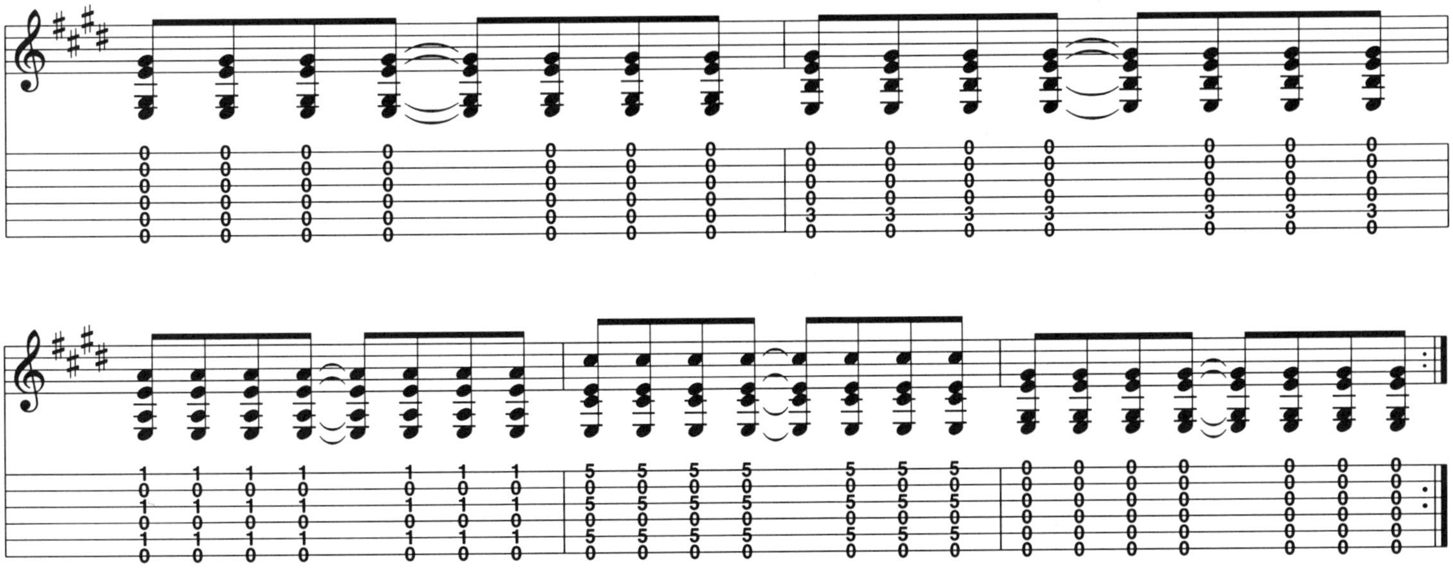

Here are some other deadly tunings in the Sonic Youth arsenal:

E E B E G♯ B on "Winner's Bone"
G G D D E♭ E♭ on "Brother James"
C C E B G D on "Cross The Breeze"
G G D D E♭ E♭ on "Cotton Crown"
F♯ F♯ G G A A on "Schizophrenia"
F♯ F♯ F♯ F♯ E B on "Kool Thing"
A C C G G♯ C on "Candle"
G G D D G G on "Teenage Riot"
E B E E A B on "Hey Joni"

Soundgarden plays many songs in alternate tunings. Taking a cue from their forebears, Sonic Youth, Soundgarden has taken the art of de-tuning to its heaviest by extensively using octaves and 5ths, and even unisons.

## E E E E E E TUNING

Talk about drone strings! Try using three octaves of E's in unison pairs. In this tuning, the ultimate E tuning (E E E E E E), the 5th string is tuned down (to match the 6th string), the 4th string is tuned up (an octave higher than the two low E's), the 3rd string is tuned down (to match the 4th string), and the 2nd string is tuned up (to match the 1st string).

Here's an example of this tuning in another melody/drone piece, this time in E Lydian (E F♯ G♯ A♯ B C♯ D♯). (A heavier 5th and 3rd string, and a lighter 2nd string might be necessary for the best possible sound.)

## E E B B B B TUNING

Soundgarden's "The Day I Tried To Live" and "My Wave" use the quintessential power-chord tuning: E E B B B B. In this tuning the 5th string is tuned down (to match the 6th string), the 4th string is tuned down (a 5th above the two low E's), the 3rd string is tuned up (to match the 2nd string), and the 1st string is tuned down to match the 2nd string. Here's an example of how Soundgarden might employ this tuning in a heavy, odd-metered riff. (Heavier 5th, 4th and 1st strings and a lighter 3rd string might be necessary for the best possible sound.)

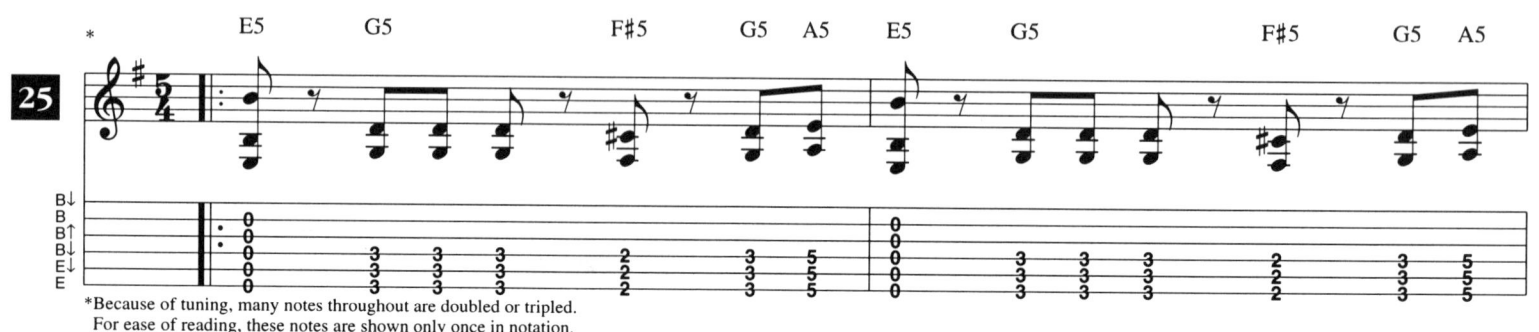

*Because of tuning, many notes throughout are doubled or tripled.
For ease of reading, these notes are shown only once in notation.
All notes actually played as shown in TAB.

These are some other Soundgarden tunings:

> B A D G B E: "Holy Water" and "Rusty Cage"
> E E B B E E: "Somewhere"
> C F C G B E: "4th Of July"
> C G C G G E: "Half"
> D G D G B C: "Like Suicide"

# ONE-SHOT TUNINGS

Here are some more one-shot tunings, and the artists who love them:

> Eb Bb Bb Gb Bb D: Smashing Pumpkins on "Mayonnaise"
> E B E E B E: Crosby, Stills and Nash on "Suite: Judy Blue Eyes"
> F A C F A C: Led Zeppelin on "When The Levee Breaks"
> C G D G Bb D: Shawn Colvin on "Tennessee"
> D D A A E E: Aerosmith on "The Other Side"
> D G C G C D: Led Zeppelin on "The Rain Song"
> D A E E A A: Michael Hedges on "All Along The Watchtower"
> D A D A C D: Van Halen on "Top Jimmy"
> C F C F A F: Led Zeppelin on "Bron-Y-Aur Stomp"
> C G D G B D: David Wilcox on "Missing You"

# SLIDE TUNINGS

The most common tunings for slide are:

> Open D Tuning—D A D F♯ A D
> Open E Tuning—E B E G♯ B E
> Open G Tuning—D G D G B D
> Open A Tuning—E A E A C♯ E
> Dobro G Tuning—G B D G B D
> D6th (Lap Steel)—D A D F♯ B D

# SLACK KEY TUNINGS

Slack key, also known as *Ki Ho Alu* and named for the "slackening" or de-tuning of the strings, originated in the early 1800s when Spanish cowboys were brought to Hawaii to control a wild cattle population explosion. Some guitars were left behind and the Hawaiians had to invent a way to play them, so they tuned the strings down until they arrived at a chord, and slack key was born. Passed down from father to son, these tunings and the songs created with them have become an integral part of modern Hawaiian music. Usually, if a player invented/discovered a tuning, it was named after him. Many recordings of the more well-known practitioners are still available—check out Gabby Pahinui, Sonny Chillingworth, Ledward Kaapana, Keola Beamer, Cyril Pahinui, and Ray Kane, all available in the world music section of your local record store. Adjusting strings, in true Hawaiian spirit, until a likable sound occurs is probably something all the artists mentioned in this book (as well as you and I) have done from time to time.

No one really knows how many slack key tunings exist, but most are based on open C, D or G.

Taro Patch (Open G)—D G D G B D
Open C—C G C G C E
Gabby C—C G E G B E
Cyril C—C G E G C E
D6/9—D A D F# B E
G Wahine—D G D F# B D
C Mauna Loa—C G E G A E

## KEOLA BEAMER-STYLE PROGRESSION

Here's an example of slack key guitar, in the style of Keola Beamer. Play the opening of bar 2 with your second finger on the 5th fret C, and your fourth finger on the 7th fret D–this is the only possible way to let the 5th fret C ring out, and be able to play the notes that follow. The harmonization of the melody in 6ths is a characteristic of the slack key tradition.

# HIGH STRUNG (NASHVILLE) TUNING

High strung tuning has been used as a production tool by Nashville producers for many years to add "sparkle" or "angel feet" to the sound of an acoustic guitar track. High strung tuning is not an alternate tuning in the traditional sense; the guitar is tuned to the same notes as in standard tuning, but the 6th, 5th, 4th and 3rd strings are tuned an octave higher. The most economical way to try Nashville tuning is to buy a 12-string set and use the octave strings on the low E, A, D and G strings (save the rest for your standard-tuned guitar). Paul Simon has used this tuning to double virtually all of his acoustic guitar parts since his Simon And Garfunkel days. This tuning is also used by David Gilmour in the opening guitar arpeggios of Pink Floyd's "Hey You."

## PINK FLOYD-STYLE PROGRESSION

This example is composed of a series of arpeggios in the key of E minor. The use of added 9ths in the Em and Am chords creates a beautifully haunting sound.

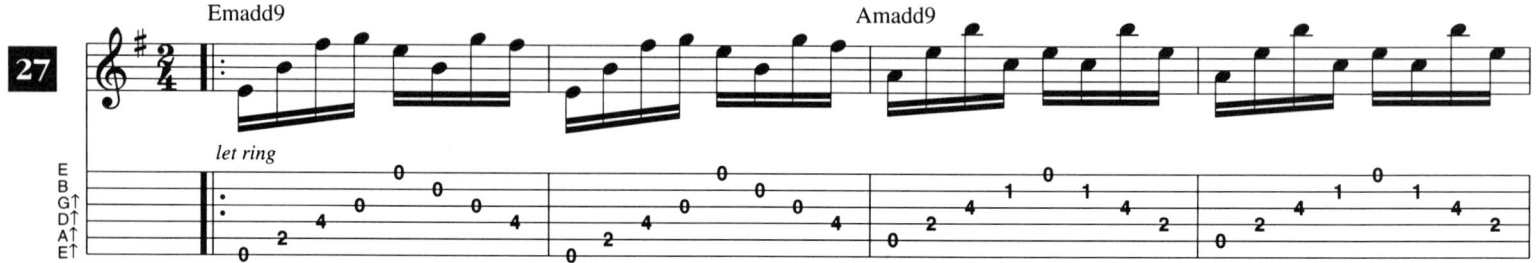

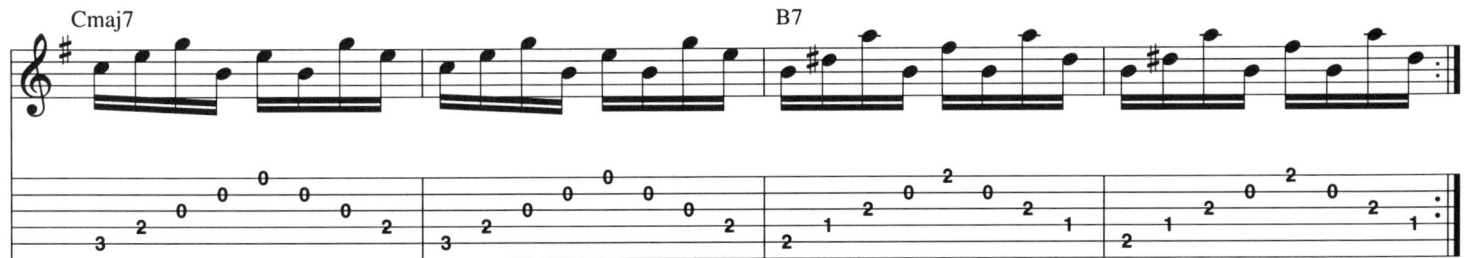

# BARITONE TUNING

Baritone tuning (B E A D F♯ B), another variation on standard tuning, requires the entire guitar to be tuned down at least a perfect 4th (2½ steps), resulting in an incredibly dense, rich texture. (True baritone guitars are usually tuned a fifth lower, sometimes even an octave lower, but such tunings are not really practical on a standard guitar.) You'll need a set of .013's, or possibly something even heavier if you can find them. Since a set of .013's still might be a little limp when tuned so far down, many guitarists prefer even heavier gauges and design their own custom sets (sometimes even using a light-gauge A [.065] from a bass set for the 6th string, and a .014 or heavier as the 1st string).

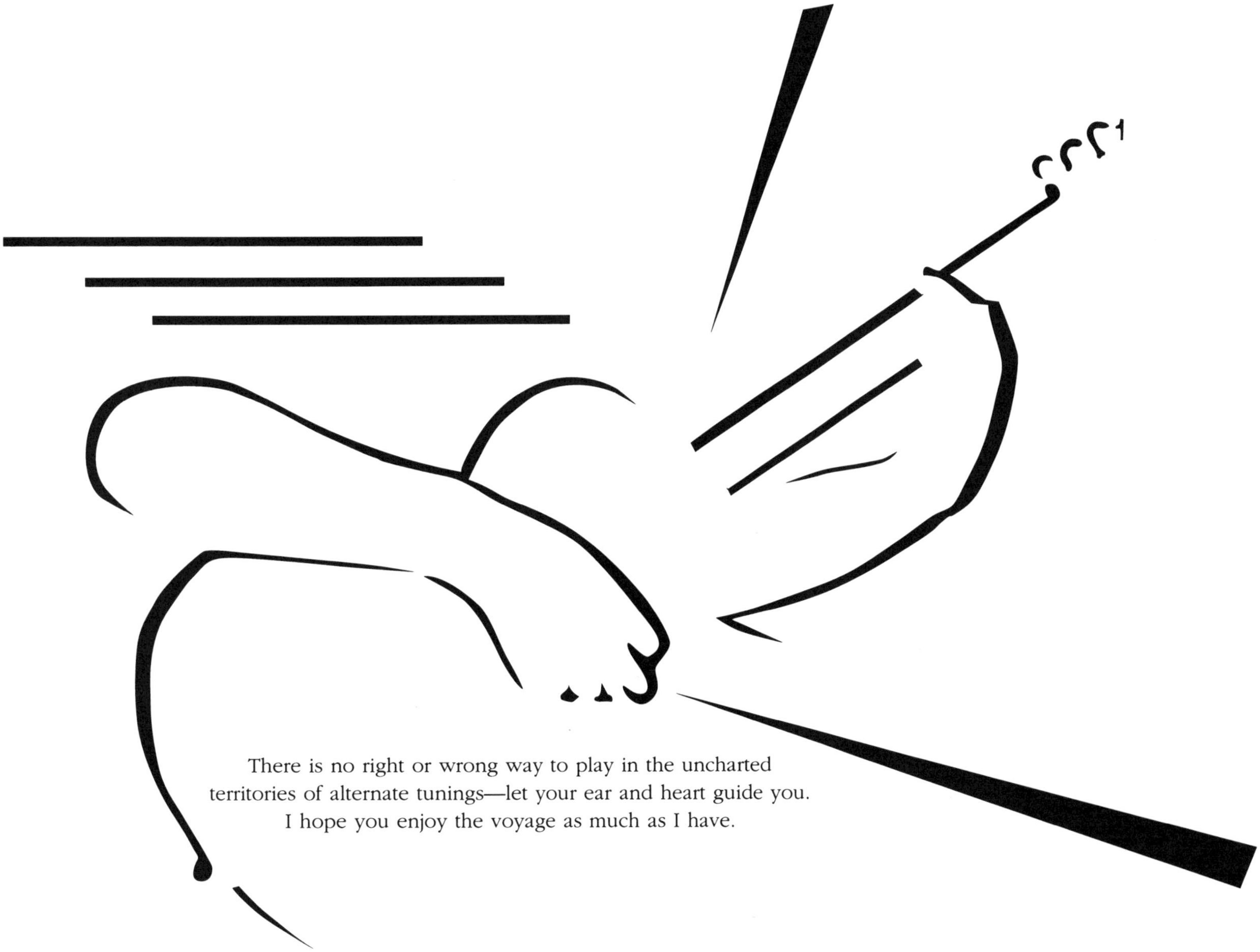

There is no right or wrong way to play in the uncharted
territories of alternate tunings—let your ear and heart guide you.
I hope you enjoy the voyage as much as I have.

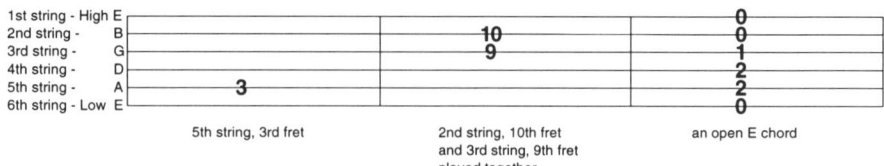

# • TABLATURE EXPLANATION/NOTATION LEGEND •

**TABLATURE:** A six-line staff that graphically represents the guitar fingerboard. By placing a number on the appropriate line, the string and the fret of any note can be indicated. For example:

```
1st string - High E
2nd string -    B
3rd string -    G
4th string -    D
5th string -    A
6th string - Low E
```

5th string, 3rd fret

2nd string, 10th fret
and 3rd string, 9th fret
played together

an open E chord

## Definitions for Special Guitar Notations

**BEND:** Strike the note and bend up ½ step (one fret).

**BEND:** Strike the note and bend up a whole step (two frets).

**BEND AND RELEASE:** Strike the note and bend up ½ (or whole) step, then release the bend back to the original note. All three notes are tied; only the first note is struck.

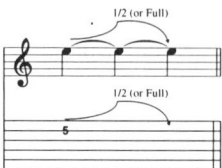

**PRE-BEND:** Bend the note up ½ (or whole) step, then strike it.

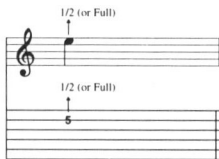

**PRE-BEND AND RELEASE:** Bend the note up ½ (or whole) step, strike it and release the bend back to the original note.

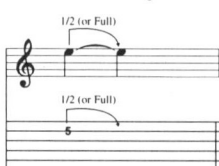

**UNISON BEND:** Strike the two notes simultaneously and bend the lower note to the pitch of the higher.

**VIBRATO:** Vibrate the note by rapidly bending and releasing the string with a left-hand finger.

**WIDE OR EXAGGERATED VI-BRATO:** Vibrate the pitch to a greater degree with a left-hand finger or the tremolo bar.

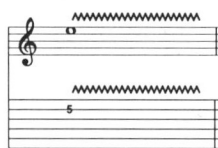

**SLIDE:** Strike the first note and then with the same left-hand finger move up the string to the second note. The second note is not struck.

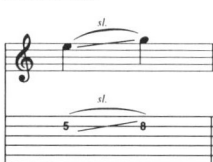

**SLIDE:** Same as above, except the second note is struck.

**SLIDE:** Slide up to the note indicated from a few frets below.

**HAMMER-ON:** Strike the first (lower) note, then sound the higher note with another finger by fretting it without picking.

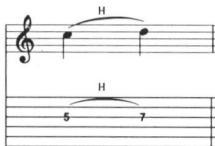

**PULL-OFF:** Place both fingers on the notes to be sounded. Strike the first (higher) note, then sound the lower note by pulling the finger off the higher note while keeping the lower note fretted.

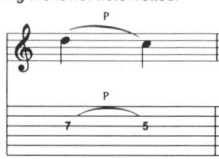

**TRILL:** Very rapidly alternate between the note indicated and the small note shown in parentheses by hammering on and pulling off.

**TAPPING:** Hammer ("tap") the fret indicated with the right-hand index or middle finger and pull off to the note fretted by the left hand.

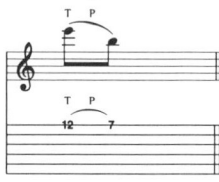

**NATURAL HARMONIC:** With a left-hand finger, lightly touch the string over the fret indicated, then strike it. A chime-like sound is produced.

**ARTIFICIAL HARMONIC:** Fret the note normally and sound the harmonic by adding the right-hand thumb edge or index finger tip to the normal pick attack.

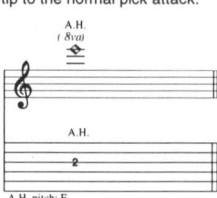

A.H. pitch: E

**TREMOLO BAR:** Drop the note by the number of steps indicated, then return to original pitch.

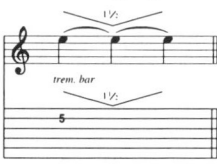

**PALM MUTE:** With the right hand, partially mute the note by lightly touching the string just before the bridge.

**MUFFLED STRINGS:** Lay the left hand across the strings without depressing them to the fret-board; strike the strings with the right hand, producing a percussive sound.

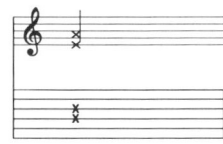

**PICK SLIDE:** Rub the pick edge down the length of the string to produce a scratchy sound.

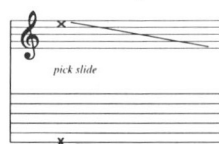

**TREMOLO PICKING:** Pick the note as rapidly and continuously as possible.

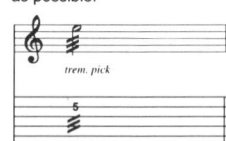

**RHYTHM SLASHES:** Strum chords in rhythm indicated. Use chord voicings found in the fingering diagrams at the top of the first page of the transcription.

**SINGLE-NOTE RHYTHM SLASHES:** The circled number above the note name indicates which string to play. When successive notes are played on the same string, only the fret numbers are given.